The Nature and Future of Christianity:
A Study of Alternative Approaches

The Nature and Future of Christianity:
A Study of Alternative Approaches

EDWARD LEROY LONG JR.

WIPF & STOCK · Eugene, Oregon

THE NATURE AND FUTURE OF CHRISTIANITY:
A STUDY OF ALTERNATIVE APPROACHES

Copyright © 2014 Edward LeRoy Long Jr. All rights reserved. Except for brief quotations in critical publications or reviews, no part of this book may be reproduced in any manner without prior written permission from the publisher. Write: Permissions, Wipf and Stock Publishers, 199 W. 8th Ave., Suite 3, Eugene, OR 97401.

Wipf & Stock
An Imprint of Wipf and Stock Publishers
199 W. 8th Ave., Suite 3
Eugene, OR 97401

www.wipfandstock.com

ISBN 13: 978-1-62564-371-1

Manufactured in the U.S.A.

Dedicated to the
Theological School of Drew University
where I concluded my teaching ministry

and to the
First Church in Oberlin, Ohio
within whose congregation I have spent more of my life
than in any other parish setting.

In both places alternative approaches can be respected.

Contents

Preface   ix

ONE   Approaches Involving the Content and Function of Beliefs   1

TWO   Seeking Personal Well-Being   17

THREE   Approaches Involving Group Identities   29

FOUR   Religious Concern for Society   43

FIVE   Rethinking Ecclesiastical Patterns   55

SIX   Interrelating Traditions   65

Concluding Reflections:
Embracing Diversity: Being Faithful Modestly   79

Bibliography   89

Preface

Something is happening to religion in our time that deserves thoughtful attention. Participation in the so-called mainline denominations is down, yet many people are moving from one faith orientation to another in a search for something that seems to more adequately address their needs and concerns. Institutional dynamics, behavioral practices, and foundational assumptions about the way to understand the human condition are all in flux. Various forms of Christianity are no exception to this state of affairs.

There is no longer any single intellectual perspective that provides the matrix for theological reflection. What is often called "modernity"—with its confidence in instrumental reason to sustain human well-being—no longer constitutes the basis on which there is a consensus about how to think about the present with assurance and look forward to the future with confidence. Claims for the uniqueness of one particular tradition are no longer persuasive as globalization confronts us with religious diversity on a scale unimaginable just a generation ago. Other religions are now practiced—not only in far away places—but by our close neighbors and associates in the workplace and in recreational encounters. Churches south of the equator—in many so-called "third world" countries—are growing, and in the process are amalgamating Christian loyalty with perspectives and cultural practices that differ from those of the Western world, which have been the vehicles for the forms of Christianity most Americans know best. Moreover, moral ideals no longer provide the basis for a unity that can be achieved apart from belief commitments. All of these developments pose challenges for persons of faith.

Preface

What is striking about the present state of reflection on these matters is how many different proposals are being advanced by those who believe religion, including Christianity, has a future and needs to be changed, or at least given new forms, in order to enjoy continued life. This diversity of approaches may be the result of increased freedom for the embrace of religion and the loss of religious authority. The door is open to almost anybody to make a suggestion or to act independently. Or it may reflect the fact that the whole field of human awareness and reflection is now much more complex than it has been in previous eras. Religion is not the only aspect of human deliberation that is marked by seemingly irreconcilable differences; differences of approach are just as severe in politics, economics, aesthetic endeavors, and even to some extent in how science and technology are to be understood and applied. Whatever the explanation, the consequences are inescapable: While it might have seemed to provide a source of unity in earlier periods of Western culture, Christianity in our time offers no single vision.

Just how massive are the pressures for diversity and change that confront us is hard to discern. Some consider them transient and temporary threats that can be overcome by a return to an imagined normalcy of the past. Others look upon them as constituting a crisis—that is, a special moment in time—that will result in as great an impact on the nature of Christian belief and practice as occurred when Eastern and Western Orthodoxy split apart in the eleventh century or when Protestantism split from the Roman Church in the sixteenth. It is not given to any of us to know with certainty how great are the stakes, yet to pay no attention to the issues or to have no engagement with their consequences is to ignore some of the most momentous challenges that confront us.

Despite this present conceptual turmoil a considerable amount of religious thinking consists of enthusiasm for some single approach that captures the imagination of its advocates, often without being examined in relationship to alternative possibilities. The result can be an uncritical embrace of a single but only partially examined possibility. This may create enthusiasm for a seemingly exciting option, but enthusiasms often have a short life and get

Preface

forgotten before they have made much of any impact or have left an enduring legacy.

In the pages that follow the primary effort will be to step back and take note of many different approaches that are currently shaping Christian faith and practice and consequently generating different visions for its possible future. Although many possibilities will be described in this overview the coverage may not be complete—the variations are too numerous and often too fleeting to permit total coverage. Nor can every option be examined thoroughly and in complete detail. But even snapshots are better than no picture at all, and awareness of the many options has more to commend it than an argument for just one possibility presented as though it could totally suffice if only everybody would embrace it.

To be sure, people are entitled to offer their own perspectives for shaping the future and should be respected when they do so. The vast range of suggested ideas deserves attention, and all of these ideas need to be considered—primarily in comparison with one another. It is very doubtful whether Christianity has ever had just one expression, and equally doubtful whether it will ever have just one form as long as many faithful, yet different, followers give it content and structure. But instead of rendering it amorphous and insignificant, this very diversity might make it exciting and rich. Being faithful should not be equated with wearing the same straitjacket even if it must include deeply trusted convictions as to what it means to be human.

Some of the approaches to be discussed in this book attract media attention and their existence is generally well known—being objects of an either favorable or unfavorable public curiosity. Some of them might be regarded as so superficial as to not merit serious attention. Other approaches to be discussed are embodied in professional theological writing that circulates primarily, if not entirely, among members of a specialized guild. There is a large amount of such writing in contemporary religious life, much of which is read only by specialists, if at all. At one time doing theology was deliberately reserved for the authoritative leaders—keeping common folk from tampering with the sacred. Most traditions have long since done away with that way of divesting the full body of believers from

Preface

a serious role, but making theology into an academic specialty may have the same shortcomings as placing reliance only in the hands of ecclesiastical officials. Unless the work of religious thinkers can be widely understood by the public little of value will be accomplished. What is especially challenging is to make the thoughts of specialists or authorities available to the rank and file of followers in ways that sustain their interest.

This book is not primarily concerned to settle the question whether or not Christianity, or any other form of religion, has a future. There may be places where addressing that question is appropriate and might even come up with plausible suggestions. The book will bracket out, or deliberately side step, this question because every proposed answer to it (either affirmative or negative) constitutes a reading of the present religious situation by those with their own set of commitments and convictions regarding the nature of that future. Such predictions tend to shed more light on the orientations of those who make them than on what will actually take place.

The characterizations of the various options treated in what follows are intended to be fair, even if admittedly brief. To cover them all exhaustively would make the book very long and crushingly weighty. Hopefully, what is presented here can prompt further study of ideas that individual readers deem to be of potential value and even perhaps lead to an enriched commitment and the candid exchange of perspectives. At least it ought to preclude any reader from quickly thinking that any single position offers an unchallenged uniqueness, complete adequacy, or unquestionable legitimacy.

When I gave the first version of this material as lectures in the adult education program of the local parish church with which I am connected, the response was "These ought to be published." Aware of the limitations inherent in covering so broad a topic in ways that are likely to be accessible to, and able to sustain the interest of, the public, I hesitated. Encouraged by the interest of these and others I have subsequently revised the lectures to make the material more suitable as a book. Professional colleagues as well as seriously concerned laity have assured me the resulting treatment

Preface

has merit whatever its limitations. A quarter century after retirement a person can take some risk. Even so, knowing that my astuteness is not what it used to be and that publishers no longer provide extensive peer evaluations or substantive editorial guidance, I have asked several friends to read the emerging drafts and help me avoid disastrous blunders. These include, listed alphabetically, Theodore Evans, Janet Fishburn, Robert Longsworth, Gregory McGonigle, Richard Simpson, Robert VanDale, and Grover Zinn. I name them to express gratitude rather than to make them hostage to whatever shortcomings remain. James Helm has helped me to ready the final submission copy in the form expected by the publisher.

If the argument of the book is correct—that no one approach to understanding Christianity is so complete as to trump all others—it follows that no one effort to state the case for that perspective is so complete as to be free of errors. Read what follows with caution.

E. L. L. Jr.
Kendal at Oberlin, Ohio
Fall 2013

ONE

Approaches Involving the Content and Function of Beliefs

Christianity, like most religions, involves both beliefs and practices. The focus of attention in this chapter is on those approaches to understanding its nature and function as centered primarily on beliefs or doctrines—that is, as offering statements about what is alleged to be true about reality. There is no question statements of truth are a very prevalent and important aspect of religious faith, although it is not all that is involved in the embrace and practice of religion. How people behave, how they treat each other in communities, and how they respond spiritually to what they take to be the Ultimate are all involved in being religious and do not necessarily correlate directly with the particular kinds of belief they embrace. Nevertheless, religious beliefs as to what is true about reality are important and a matter of concern—even a matter of disagreement—today as they have been throughout the course of Christian history.

In looking at Christian beliefs attention must be directed to two matters. The first involves the content of particular beliefs. Do religious beliefs make assertions that correspond with reality? Are they to be taken as descriptive in the direct sense, such as many people think scientific ideas are, or are they interpretative characterizations that are more analogous to poetic portrayals of meaning, the validity of which is legitimate on very different grounds? Do they belong somewhere between these two contrasting options? The second factor to be considered in understanding religious doctrines concerns their legitimization. By what criteria are they to be alleged to be true or decisively useful? Can they be legitimized on the basis of ordinary reason, that is, the modes of thought and inquiry that are present in a given cultural setting, or is their significance confined to the special community of devotion whose premises are different from those of the prevailing culture? If religious beliefs are legitimized only within communities of faith does this render them inaccessible to others?

In looking at contemporary versions of Christianity in which doctrinal correctness plays a major role many people would probably bring to mind Protestant fundamentalism and Roman Catholic orthodoxy. Both seem to place much emphasis on what they assert to be true about reality—both natural and supernatural. Both place great weight upon the truth status of doctrine and both utilize the term "infallibility" to establish the alleged validity of religious assertions. They tend to think of the Christian tradition as consisting of unchanging beliefs that correctly point to what is true.

Protestant fundamentalism claims to be "the faith once for all delivered unto the saints." However, its listing of the specific set of beliefs by which it determines what is orthodox faith was only created between 1910 and 1912—primarily as a reaction to an emerging view of Christianity known as modernism. Almost every major Protestant denomination has seen some of its adherents embrace fundamentalism and some denominations (most notably Southern Baptists and Missouri Synod Lutherans) have experienced it as a dominant, often even controlling, influence. The term "fundamentalist" should not be used carelessly, for it is not applicable to all evangelicals, or to most so called mega-churches, nor even to classical orthodoxy. None of the great figures in church history—such as Augustine, Aquinas, Luther, Calvin, Jonathan Edwards, Charles Finney—would recognize themselves by that term. Fundamentalism as originally conceived declares that five basic beliefs are essential to orthodoxy: the first and most emphasized of these is the assertion of biblical inerrancy. From this follows the claim that both

Approaches Involving the Content and Function of Beliefs

the biblical stories of creation and the miracles of Jesus are records of historical events, that Christ was born of a Virgin, that there will be a bodily resurrection and a second coming of Christ, and that the substitutionary theory of the atonement (the bloody one!) is the right and proper view. Making these the touchstones of correct Christian belief was a modern development.

Much Roman Catholicism shares the view that in order to be reliable Christian dogma must be continuous and correct. It locates responsibility for ensuring that to be the case by speaking of the church's tradition as the source of guidance. But since that tradition is complex and sometimes marked by differences, the pope is taken to be the guardian of the heritage and alleged to have the power to speak infallibly. This way of insuring orthodoxy was formally and categorically declared to be decisive only in 1870, when the concept of papal infallibility was affirmed by the First Vatican Council as having always been operative in the tradition. Moreover, the use of the concept to make a specific matter of belief binding occurred only some eighty years later when the promulgation of the dogma regarding the bodily assumption of Mary was declared to be a necessary article of faith. No other item of required belief has been made binding by the explicit use of the concept of papal infallibility.

Both of these appeals to infallibility are reactive and essentially modern responses to developments that were regarded at the time as threats to faith. Both are reactions to the challenges posed to religious faith by a way of thinking known as the Enlightenment. Hence, these are late developments within the Christian tradition, meaning that at least in a chronological sense they are modern. Nevertheless, they exercise a great influence and tend to give the impression that Christian doctrine is difficult to reconcile with Enlightenment ways of thinking about the nature of reality.

What many people, both those who embrace the idea of infallibility and those who reject it, often fail to realize is that both of these approaches create something like a proof to vindicate faith. This means they tend to place prior and therefore decisive confidence in the assertion used to legitimate faith rather than in the claim of faith itself. To rely on something lesser than God to legitimize belief in God might very well be to construct an idol.

Fortunately for the viability and future of theology these assertions of infallibility do not exhaust the ways in which Christians deal with the nature and future of belief. Many contemporary Christians understand the function of beliefs in quite different ways.

Other Responses to the Challenge of Modernity

Thinking about the formulation and function of Christian beliefs in the thought world of modernity has been a major preoccupation of much contemporary theology. In the 1930s a German New Testament scholar, Rudolf Bultmann, suggested the need to release the central affirmations of the gospel from the categories in which it has been historically set forth. Bultmann's approach came to be understood as demythologizing. It involves trying to restate the significance of Christ and his work without relying on the thought patterns in which it is traditionally enmeshed in both the Bible and in most traditional Christian thinking. The traditional approach that Bultmann found problematic involved a three-tiered world (heaven above, earth in the middle, and hell below), the acceptance of miracles, supernatural intervention in nature, and belief in a final judgment at the end of history. Bultmann contended that the significance of Christ's work could be affirmed without being tied to these "myths." This proposal has been met both with resistance and with complex efforts to use it to come up with ways of understanding Christian faith in the modern world.

Many efforts to do this lay somewhere between two poles. One of these, that of Drew Emeritus Professor Thomas Oden, seeks to recapture the essence of Christian orthodoxy by returning to a study of its early expression in the writings of the apostolic fathers. Many of Oden's books deal with matters of general interest, like the Wesleyan heritage, the pastoral care of souls, the nature of ministry, and even the humor of Kierkegaard. The books most pertinent to our inquiry, which were written later in his career and which set forth his theological identity toward the conclusion of his career, include: *Agenda for Theology, Turning Around the Mainline,* and *The Rebirth of Orthodoxy.* Oden is neither a fundamentalist nor a

Approaches Involving the Content and Function of Beliefs

Catholic in the Roman sense, but he is suspicious of the significance and value of modernity as a worldview and has come to be generally thought of as a theological conservative.

In the first of these books, *Agenda for Theology* (the dust jacket of which bears the subtitle *Recovering Christian Roots*, and which was published in 1979), Oden does two things: first, he indicates why in his judgment (which he alleges is shared by many of his students and other associates) "modernity"—his term for the intellectual climate nurtured by the Enlightenment—no longer offers a satisfying and dependable understanding of the human situation. According to Oden "modernity persists in fantasizing history as a progressive evolution toward ever better forms wherein our most vexing mortal ills will finally be cured though improved education, technology, and moral suasion."[1] To believe that, Oden contends, is to wear ideological blinders.

According to Oden, most current theological responses—he calls them fads—have adopted the premises of modernity in order to speak to it. They have been and are increasingly proving to be unsuccessful. Therefore, Oden makes his second move, which is to assert that

> If we are to understand [Christianity's] original meaning and value we must come again to see it through the eyes of those who have had to struggle for it and maintain it. It is from the martyrs, saints, and prophets of Christian history, more than from recent riskless [sic] interpreters, that we can learn the value of classical Christianity. Without their instruction, Christianity becomes a mere recollection, a bored nodding of the head, the source of an occasional laugh, or, in an emergency, an item to pawn.[2]

Four years later Oden published *The Rebirth of Orthodoxy*, a book that elaborated and substantially added to the proposal advanced in the *Agenda for Theology*. In it he gives an autobiographical account of his personal transition from a liberal thinker to one whose outlook is indebted to Christian reflection as discovered in

---

1. Oden, *Agenda for Theology*, 164.
2. Ibid., 2.

the early church fathers. He also again asserts impressionistically that he finds both his students and many of his professional associates making the same transition he has made—a shift that Oden argues will become normative in the future of the church.

According to Oden, the orthodox tradition supplies depth and meaning that current trends in theology are not providing. Orthodoxy, as Oden defines it—using an ancient rule from Vincent of Lerins—is that understanding of faith held "by everyone, everywhere, and at all times." Of course, Oden acknowledges that from time to time there have been periodic examples of minority departures from the tradition, but he believes these have proven temporary and have been discredited by the deliberative actions of the church because they have been judged to be either inadequate or heretical.

In contrast, Oden's contemporary, John Shelby Spong, who was once the Episcopal Bishop of Newark, New Jersey, argues that the future of Christianity depends upon the embrace of modern ways of thinking rather than their repudiation. Many laypersons interested in theology seem to be more familiar with Spong's views than with Oden's, though this may be only my own impressionistic observation.

Spong's relationship to the question before us is apparent in the titles of two of his books. The first, published in 1998, is called *Why Christianity Must Change or Die*. The second, published five years later is *A New Christianity for a New World*. Spong is a clear, forceful, and zealous exponent of the view that Christian beliefs must be reconceptualized in order to be relevant to a modern world.

Spong started his journey to this outlook when he was the rector of an Episcopal parish in Richmond, Virginia. He and a rabbi from a local synagogue encountered each other in public sessions dealing with the relationships between the two traditions. This forced him to reconsider his own convictions, and particularly those shaped by his early years in southern Protestant conservatism (which Spong describes as fundamentalist). Spong began his journey toward radical liberalism when reading the book *Honest to God* by the Anglican bishop John A. T. Robinson. That book acknowledges the fact that traditional theism has lost its credibility for

Approaches Involving the Content and Function of Beliefs

many and needs to be modified. Spong increasingly found himself prompted to become a spokesman for those who want to believe in some form of ultimate meaning but are turned off "by the premodern literalism that so frequently masquerades as Christianity."[3]

The central portion of Spong's book is devoted to reconceptualizing traditional theological ideas. One chapter indicates how we can/should move beyond traditional theism to new images for thinking about God. After a long examination of the inadequacy of traditional theism, Spong argues that we must break out of the personalistic images that we commonly use to think about God. He appeals to the theology of Paul Tillich, among others, for understanding God in terms of being itself—the ground and the essential quality of existence. This brief excerpt illustrates how Spong endorses such thinking:

> There is no God external to life. God, rather, is the inescapable depth and center of all that is. God is not a being superior to all other beings. God is the Ground of Being itself. And much flows from this starting place. The artifacts of the past must be understood in a new way if they are to accompany us beyond the exile [Spong uses the term "exile" to signify modern doubt], and those that cannot be understood differently will have to be laid aside.[4]

In dealing with Jesus, a task to which Spong devotes several chapters, he suggests that we must do away with the superstitious and mysterious aura with which the church has surrounded him (an aura sustained by a scriptural literalism untenable in the eyes of modern scholarship) and concentrate on the experience with Jesus that the early disciples had. (Spong draws on the work of a group of New Testament scholars, called the Jesus Seminar, as his rationale for doing this). In a sharp disavowal of ideas central to many Christians, Spong also argues that the image of Jesus as the "divine rescuer" has to be discarded—along with such doctrines as original sin and human depravity. These doctrines buttress belief in the need for that kind of redemption. Instead we should experience Jesus as a "spirit person" through which a fully human person

---

3. Spong, *Why Christianity Must Change*, xvii.
4. Ibid., 70.

entered into divinity rather than as a divine being who became temporarily human.

Spong does not offer as extended a reconceptualization of the third person of the Trinity as he offers with respect to the idea of God and the significance of Jesus, but rather ends the book with chapters on prayer, ethics, the church, and eternal life. He is not sure that his approach will eventually be accepted either by the church as a faith community or even by those in the world of "church refugees" who think Christianity needs to be jettisoned altogether, but he does believe it provides the only possible hope for the future.

Spong's second book, *A New Christianity for a New World*, does not differ greatly from the previous book, but argues the themes with greater elaboration and more strident intensity. Consider this brief passage from near the end of the book:

> [In this new approach] Christianity becomes not something to be believed but a faith into which we must live, a vision that stands before us, inviting us to enter. I proclaim a God beyond creeds, a Christ beyond incarnation, a way of life that dares to grasp the insecurities of our being and move beyond the boxes created by the security-producing churches of yesterday. To be ready to move into this not fully clear vision is to face honestly the recognition that the place where the church, with its binding creeds and closed scriptures, has traditionally dwelt is no longer a livable place. If we vote to stay we vote to die.[5]

Although this passage seems to suggest that belief is no longer the decisive factor in thinking about the nature of Christianity, it is primarily a declaration of belief.

It is probably hard for those whose experiences with Christianity are in those traditions that think of religious fidelity as determined by doctrinal assertions about the nature of reality to understand how an Episcopal bishop could venture forth ideas seemingly at such odds with the usual understanding of the tradition. Episcopalian piety centers on its liturgical practice far more than on specific doctrinal assertions. To those who invest the time

---

5. Ibid., 243f.

Approaches Involving the Content and Function of Beliefs

and commitments to this set of practices, the result is acculturation that is deeply satisfying on an affective level, and that allows for the toleration of cognitive differences, which less liturgical communities only look upon as involving heresy.

Anyone who has been through or is still grounded in what is called liberal Christianity will find much of what Spong suggests to be quite familiar, though restated with verve and emphasis in the context of the twenty-first rather than the middle of the twentieth century. Spong is moving in almost complete counter directions from Oden in respect to the substance of faith assertions. Yet underneath and in some respects they may have quite a bit in common. There are several incidental similarities with no major significance. For instance, they both resided in New Jersey when developing their ideas; both write in a style that is easily grasped by laity as well as professionals; both utilize personal and autobiographical considerations in their writing. But there are other and perhaps more significant similarities. Both are repudiating an earlier period in their faith journey. Oden came to Drew as an avowed liberal wearing beads and long hair. Spong has spent much of his life repudiating the conservatism of his southern upbringing. Both were prompted to take a new look at their early stance through encounters with Jewish scholars; both employ considerable invective in their writing; and most of all, both seem to understand religious statements as signifying reality directly. Their difference seems to be basically about the reality to which theological statements should point.

The issue highlighted by the contrast between these two writers is how Christianity is to deal with so-called modernity—that is, a thought world dominated by Enlightenment rationality and reliance upon empirical sources of knowledge. That issue is not entirely new. From its very beginning Christianity, like many other worldviews, has used the categories of understanding current at any time to formulate its message. The question this has always raised, and continues to be raised today, is whether those categories function merely as vehicles for Christianity's understanding of reality or whether by employing them a faith system is locked into a specific

The Nature and Future of Christianity

worldview that is at odds with the Christian faith. If it does not use the thought forms of its day Christianity probably cannot communicate its views to others; if by using them it gives up some essential facet of its convictions, its legitimacy as an understanding of reality may be fundamentally distorted.

While Oden and Spong represent contrasting responses to Bultmann's challenge, many contemporary theologians are working somewhere in the middle between such sharply different poles. They approach Christianity as a system of beliefs and seek to commend the central affirmations of the faith in ways that are compatible with modernity's suspicion of "myths," yet they remain committed to the premise that Christian faith involves beliefs about the nature of reality and how human beings are related to God and the saving work of Christ. The task of doing this can be daunting and the result is that some of the efforts to do this are set forth in massive writings read only by professionals.

In his book *Message and Existence: An Introduction to Christian Theology*, which was written primarily to be a guide for the non-professional, Professor Langdon Gilkey of the University of Chicago takes pains to explain that we must understand how religious language functions in order to appreciate the truth of traditional doctrinal ideas. Gilkey is aware of the difficulty of rendering theological discourse accessible to the average contemporary reader, and is correct in observing that much theology is difficult for the average Christian believer to grasp. Basically his understanding of doctrinal thinking is analogical—that is, it affirms the importance of language to point to realities that are clearly substantial and real, but that are misunderstood when that language is understood literally rather than symbolically. According to Gilkey

> Our words about God as not literal, direct, or univocal (that is, used in precisely the same way) in relation to God because of the divine transcendence; also, they are not empty, meaningless, or "equivocal" because of the essential and recognizable activity of God in the world of our experience. Rather, our words are analogical or symbolic—words which in some respects apply and in others do not. . . .

Approaches Involving the Content and Function of Beliefs

To speak directly or literally of God is to imply that God is an object or entity in the universe and essentially (metaphysically), therefore, similar to other entities. In such a case God ceases to be "God" as a transcendent yet related creator and preserver.[6]

How the analogical use of language applies to the many other Christian doctrines is a long and complex story seldom broached in the limited parameters of Christian worship and education. Many contemporary theologians realize that the uses of theological terminology and concepts involve ways of understanding that seldom filter down to the ordinary parish setting. This is unfortunate because significant affirmations of meaning can be conveyed in language that functions symbolically rather than literally. Moreover, the symbolic use of language is evident in other contexts. For instance, patriotic stories, like those of George Washington and the cherry tree, or children's fables like those of Santa Claus, are used in ways that everyone understands and continues to use in what amounts to a process of demythologizing, even though it is not given that name. The narratives of biblical faith are often couched in similar kinds of discourse, though they may seem more plausible as descriptive statements (and sometimes are). But to read them only as literal assertions may be to miss the profounder ways in which they can function as affirmations of meaning.

It is important to recognize that the movement to rethink the nature of Christian beliefs of which the figures I have used as contrasting examples has many more participants, some of which may be even better known. It includes some scholars, like Marcus Borg and Walter Brueggemann, whose primary field of expertise is biblical studies. The approach of these many figures varies in detail but all of them are devoutly concerned to understand Christianity is a way that offers promise for its continued viability. It also includes thinkers like John Cobb and, Catherine Keller who observe the natural and the historical processes that go on around us and construct meaningful affirmations pointing to their significance and sustaining qualities.

---

6. Gilkey, *Message and Existence*, 102.

The Nature and Future of Christianity

An Alternative Way of Understanding the Function of Doctrine

There is yet another understanding of the role of beliefs. It points out that doctrines have other roles to play than to serve as descriptions of reality or even affirmations of meaning. Perhaps the clearest and most challenging illustration of this approach can be found in a book by Professor George Lindbeck of Yale Divinity School called *The Nature of Doctrine: Religion and Theology in a Postliberal Age*. This is difficult reading—not only because it is printed in the small type that publishers are increasingly using to save paper—but because it is conceptually challenging. It does not use the kind of ordinary terminology that we down-to-earth types find easy to understand. Nevertheless, it has been hailed as groundbreaking because it takes into account the function of language as it is being thought about by anthropologists, sociologists, and contemporary philosophers and applies those understandings to how we should think about the nature and function of doctrinal assertions.

Lindbeck's book does not argue for one set of beliefs over and against another (as both Oden and Spong do) but asks how doctrines function in the life of religious communities. The text is somewhat dense, as is evident in this short selection that summarizes what the book attempts to do.

> [In this book] emphasis is placed on those respects in which religions resemble languages together with their correlative forms of life and are similar to cultures (in so far as these are understood semiotically as reality and value systems—that is, as idioms for the constructing of reality and for the living of life). The function of church doctrines that becomes most prominent in this perspective is their use, not as expressive symbols or as truth claims, but as communally authoritative rules of discourse, attitude and action. This general way of conceptualizing religion will be called in what follows a "a cultural-linguistic" approach, and the implied view of church doctrine will be referred to as a "regulative" or "rule" theory.[7]

---

7. Lindbeck, *The Nature of Doctrine*, 17f.

Approaches Involving the Content and Function of Beliefs

Perhaps the quickest and possibly easiest way to realize what is being proposed is to take a specific example of how Lindbeck deals with a rather familiar religious doctrine—namely, the doctrine of papal infallibility. This is typically understood as declaring the pope is correct in what he declares to be proper belief. When used that way it means the pope cannot be wrong. Lindbeck reinterprets the doctrine to be a rule for the community that accepts the pope as the final authority whose judgment is to be followed in case the community is caught in disagreements or controversies that cannot be settled by other means. Although Lindbeck is a Lutheran, he also applies this approach Christology and Mariology. All this is in a book with the imprint of a Presbyterian publisher!

To think about belief in God according to this understanding would be to abandon the idea that God is an actual reality who sits somewhere in the stratosphere where he might be hit by a space satellite. Understood functionally, God is a concept that focuses the value and identity of a community beyond itself and also (though this idea is biblical rather than typical of most contemporary thinking) God is the concept that prompts a community to be humbly grateful for its very being and to acknowledge its own shortcomings and moral inadequacies.

Perhaps the impact of Lindbeck's approach can be understood by suggesting a thought experiment. The following conjectural illustration is mine, not his, but it is an example of how his idea might work out if utilized to deal with the doctrine of election. There is probably no doctrine that is regarded by theological liberals or idealistic rationalists as more repulsive. Might Lindbeck's method rescue such a doctrine from being hard-hearted dogmatism?

The idea of election acknowledges the fact that some people have faith and some do not. If this is understood as indicating an arbitrary choice by God it can quite rightly be judged to be a cruel idea—an idea that prompts many to turn to a universalism that leaves nobody out. But understood as a description of human responses to the question of Ultimacy it may even make some empirical sense. There simply is no set of discernible reasons that fully explains why some people are believers and some are not. In arriving at worldviews people don't simply line up the evidence and decide on the basis of some rational objectivity what is factually correct. Indeed, they probably cannot do that because the very reasoning employed when dealing with such matters is already shaped by the conclusion that is embraced. Augustine suggested this when he said we believe first and then understand—which contrasts with the more rational assumption that we first understand and then derive or test faith by that stance.

The underlying assumption of the idea of election is that faith is a divinely instigated gift rather than the result of a human decision. At one time this doctrine was used to argue against efforts at evangelistic conversion. It might be more appropriately used in a pluralistic culture to argue that conceptual assaults on those who come to different decisions about faith are illegitimate. Such assaults—whether by believers against nonbelievers or by nonbelievers against believers—assume religious convictions are matters for which individuals are entirely responsible and they can and ought to be changed by the use of compelling arguments, or perhaps even coercive pressures.

To refrain from conceptual assaults, however, need not preclude sharing convictions and bearing witness to one's faith, but it does rule contemptuous criticisms of others out of order. If worldviews are not simply expressions or products of merely rational deliberation then they cannot be treated as a form of intellectual malfeasance. This means that we are to accept those whose views on matters of faith differ from our own and even from the dictates of a religious authority. Applied as a rule for the behavior of a religious community the idea of election can therefore legitimize the acceptance of diversity—perhaps even more substantively than a simpler idea of tolerance. End of the thought experiment.

There is probably no escaping the realization that religion does attempt to offer conceptual understandings of reality and that when it does so its assertions are heard by those whose thinking is shaped by the thought world that surrounds them. Religious formulations that come to us from various cultures of the past are impossible to understand from the standpoint of a subsequently developed linear cognitive rationalism that regards all statements as literally descriptive of reality. As moderns we are not well trained to think

Approaches Involving the Content and Function of Beliefs

in terms that carry symbolic meanings yet when we speak of how to think of our country and its heritage we often rely on language that functions differently than do statements of so-called facts. When we seek to express affections we often employ metaphor and even hyperbole as well as descriptive terms. The cause of faith understanding would be advanced if the process of catechizing for the faith included sophisticated explanations of the nature and function of religious language and not merely instruction in its content.

TWO

Seeking Personal Well-Being

A second way of understanding the role of Christian faith is oriented toward the improvement of personal fortune or experience. There is no doubt but what the Bible speaks of something like "the fullness of life," and it does suggest that there are benefits to be had from living faithfully. It is not surprising that a number of approaches to Christianity—most of them modern—build on that promise, even if by doing so they run the danger of overlooking the conditions the Bible tells us are necessary for being blessed by such benefits.

From Positive Thinking to the Prosperity Gospel

Two clergymen who held membership in the Reformed Church of America played pivotal roles in characterizing the significance of religious faith as a source of personal well-being. This small denomination (colloquially identified as the Dutch Reformed Church) sprang out of Calvinistic roots. Though neither Norman Vincent Peale or Robert Schuller are typical of that denomination, neither of them severed their connection to it, nor did the public realize the irony involved in the fact that their approach to Christianity was almost the direct antithesis of that of the Reformed heritage. Even so, unlike many of the figures who later built on their way of

The Nature and Future of Christianity

understanding the Christian message as a source of personal well-being, both of them wore Geneva gowns when preaching.

Norman Vincent Peale, after serving several Methodist churches, became pastor of the Marble Collegiate Church in New York City. He is best known for espousing the power of positive thinking, which is the title of a book he wrote that sold some five million copies. He also wrote *The Art of Living: A Guide to Confident Thinking* and *The Tough Minded Optimist*, as well as many other publications. These titles characterize the nature of the preaching he did both from the pulpit and over the radio—a message portraying religion as a guide to self assurance and personal well-being. Peale also pioneered cooperation with psychologists and psychiatrists in providing personal counseling under religious auspices—counseling aimed at overcoming personal difficulties.

Peale's approach was not without its detractors—from both the scientific and theological communities. Many felt it ignored the social issues of the day by reconfiguring religion into a self-help mechanism. Peale avoided the controversy between so-called modernists and fundamentalists that was dividing so many churches in his day over doctrinal matters. He did so by utilizing an entirely different set of categories for portraying what it means to have religious faith. Although his thinking seemed to deal entirely with personal aspects of faith, he opposed the presidential aspiration of Adlai Stevenson because he was divorced and of John F. Kennedy because he was a Roman Catholic. He was also vocal advocate of American intervention in the effort to stem the Nazi threat to France and England in the early forties when many church leaders were pacifists.

By the time Robert Schuller became an active public figure television had replaced radio as the primary means by which this religious approach was given wide publicly. His weekly broadcast, "The Hour of Power," often featured interviews with figures known for their achievements in worldly endeavors. He built a huge sanctuary in Orange County California known as the Crystal Cathedral and to a large extent simply avoided any mention of the controversial social issues that were troublesome at the time.

Seeking Personal Well-Being

The approach to Christian faith pioneered by Peale and Schuller would greatly expand in the years that followed, often in so called mega-churches that were built around the personalities of their leaders—now almost always stripped of Geneva gowns and attired in either business attire or even something casual. Positive thinking both offers the power to succeed and implies divine sanction for doing so, and thereby tends to approve of the typically American version of success translated into religious entrepreneurship. To be sure, not all popular media religious figures who attained notoriety have built on the model created by the positive thinkers. Radio and television preachers now include fundamentalists, evangelists in the more traditional sense, and some self-promoters as well as spokespersons for personal well-being. Few of them are affiliated with any historically organized denomination. Nevertheless, the heritage of Peale and Schuller is now carried on by leaders with similar or analogous orientations, of which Oral Roberts, Joel Osteen, and Bishop Eddie Long would probably be the most widely known examples.

Oral Roberts fits into this model in his own special way. Raised in the Pentecostal tradition, he was convinced by reading the Bible that it is all right with God to be rich. He developed a television ministry using the term "seed faith" and founded an evangelistic association bearing his name, which raised considerable sums to fund both a college and a medical center. In the latter part of his ministry he became a United Methodist though he did not make much change in his message. Although most commentators think of him as laying the foundation for what latter became known as the prosperity gospel, his major emphasis was on faith healing, and he placed considerable emphasis on the cultivation of personal sanctity in a conventional, middle class lifestyle. Roberts, whose evangelistic achievements are sometimes regarded as secondary in importance only to those of Billy Graham, did not make concern for social justice a major focus of his message, yet those who came under his influence have tended to view Christianity's relationship to society in conservative terms.

The Nature and Future of Christianity

Joel Osteen, who studied two years at Oral Roberts University, began his career as the television producer for the services of his father's church, the Lakewood Baptist Church in Houston, Texas. He then succeeded his father as pastor. His first book bears the title *Your Best Hope Now: 7 Steps to Living at Your Full Potential* and was published in 2004. He has traveled to many countries with his message and has written a second book *Becoming a Better You: 7 Steps to Improving Your Life Everyday*, which is reported to have sold four million copies. Osteen has appeared frequently on news broadcasts and was designated "The Most Influential Christian in America" by *The Church Report* in 2006. While Osteen preaches the legitimacy of affluence he is not as prone as many other right wing figures to strongly condemn homosexuality or Mormonism. Like other proponents of the prosperity gospel social justice is not his main emphasis.

Both the term "prosperity gospel" and the related term "the health and wealth gospel" contend that the chief function and future of religion is to improve the worldly fortunes of individuals, often in monetary terms. The advocates of this approach base their message on biblical texts that commend the diligent use of talents as the defining feature of faithful living. The emphasis is one of positive optimism. Biblical texts that raise questions about the acquisition and love of possessions are conveniently ignored.

Some of the congregations in which this approach is central hold seminars on financial responsibility and thus seemingly embrace a moral concern, but a Duke University professor who has studied these programs reports that they encourage the acquisition of expensive possessions, and another author has argued that they have had a role in creating the housing bubble in the recent financial meltdown. Those observations may be a bit exaggerated, but there is certainly no doubt this kind of Christianity panders to individualized self-aggrandizement in a way that bears very little, if any, resemblance to the main tradition's understanding of the Bible. The fact that three of the four largest congregations in America embrace this approach suggests the power of its appeal in our society.

Seeking Personal Well-Being

The Purpose Driven Life

Efforts to understand the function of religion as a way to improve personal experience may not be as individualistic as those just described. Rick Warren takes the concern for personal well-being in somewhat different directions. Warren is the founding pastor of the Saddleback Church in Lake Forest, California. His book, *The Purpose Driven Life: What on Earth Am I Here For?*, has sold some thirty million copies. He also has a website he uses to further his approach. Satellite churches inspired by this idea have arisen in many parts of the country. Warren's book is fully infused with biblical references. It cites some 715 biblical verses (according to a count of the citations in the back). While citing Scripture does not guarantee a wise or valid understanding of the biblical worldview, it is clear that Warren aims to give the Bible a serious place in his thinking.

Warren's book begins by claiming:

> This is more than a book; it is guide to a *40-day spiritual journey* that will enable you to discover the answer to life's most important question: What on earth am I here for? By the end of this journey you will know God's purpose for your life and will understand the big picture—how all the pieces of your life fit together. Having this perspective will reduce your stress, simplify your decisions, increase your satisfaction, and, most important, prepare you for eternity.[1]

The main body of the book is divided into forty chapters, with the suggestion to the reader to read one each day and pause to consider its implications. The forty-day format corresponds in length to the pilgrimages taken by both Moses and Jesus. The six main sections of Warren's book, listed below, contain seven proposed daily reflections, the titles of which provide a sense of the book's focus.

---

1. Warren, *The Purpose Driven Life*, 9.

The Nature and Future of Christianity

WHAT ON EARTH AM I HERE FOR?

PURPOSE #1: You Were Planned for God's Pleasure

PURPOSE #2: You Were Formed for God's Family

PURPOSE #3: You Were Created to Become Like Christ

PURPOSE #4: You Were Shaped for Serving God

PURPOSE #5: You Were Made for a Mission

While these headings direct attention to personal well-being, Warren's understanding of faith and its purposes is somewhat different from that of the prosperity gospel. For instance, his treatment of Purpose #2 is especially important because it indicates that although Warren is concerned with the way religion changes personal experience, he is not bound to the stark individualism of some other exponents of this view. According to Warren, we are created as human beings but we become God's children only by being in his family. Doing so involves inheriting a rich legacy that is "priceless, pure, permanent, and protected."[2] This can never be taken away from us. This involves being baptized, learning how to live unselfishly, laying aside the busyness that gets in the way of being related to one another, and giving ourselves to others, beginning right now.

This means religion as Warren understands it involves being in community. The word "church" comes into this discussion—but mainly (if not indeed only) for its significance as a fellowship that helps people to develop "spiritual muscle," engage in mission, avoid backsliding behavior, and share experience with others.[3] Sharing with others involves giving and receiving life with them, and experiencing sympathy, mercy, and forgiveness. All of this can be sensed only by those who are wholeheartedly focused on what it means to bind people together. Further, doing this means avoiding gossip and practicing conflict resolution. Warren points out that this has worked successfully at Saddleback Church—and judging from the statistics, he is possibly right.

2. Ibid., 119.
3. Ibid., 134–37.

Much of what Warren writes reflects significant elements of traditional Christianity but almost entirely shorn of the terminology associated with the tradition. Is the loss of that terminology something to worry about or is it the key to success in speaking about religious matters to contemporary suburban American culture? Nobody can be sure. It does lend itself to lifestyles such as those associated with the prosperity gospel—but there is much more to it than that, even though its title suggests that religion is primarily something achieved by human effort and works from the human to the divine rather than being something that by grace moves from the divine to the human. This turns the canard of extreme Calvinism—willingness to be damned for the glory of God—completely around and embraces belief in God as a means of making human well-being more glorious.

While Warren avoids the problematic consequences that can stem from the crass embrace of the prosperity gospel, he may not account sufficiently for the complexities, ambiguities, and inescapable entanglements in malfeasance that characterize the social process. His view of sin might not satisfy a Calvinist, nor is his view of salvation characterized by a rich sense of gratitude for redeeming grace. It models religious fidelity more on the model of success rather than on a model of confession and forgiveness. The pictures of Warren show him dressed in business casual; he doesn't wear a Geneva gown!

Christianity as Spirituality rather than Belief

The third example of the approaches under this heading is a book by Harvey Cox, the author of the once bestselling book *The Secular City*, which argued the case for viewing the future of religion as being bleak—having a diminished role in the face of a robust rationality marked by intellectual openness. There were other thinkers at the time suggesting the same idea, one phrase for which was religion-less Christianity. Cox has subsequently written a book with the title *The Future of Faith*, which views what is happening in the religious scene somewhat differently than did his previous outlook.

The Nature and Future of Christianity

Cox is an informed and capable scholar, a superb writer of easily grasped arguments, and an astute observer of what is the prevalent cultural *zeitgeist*. His book is interlaced with passages about his own spiritual odyssey—which runs the gamut from being brought up as a Baptist in the suburbs of Philadelphia, to having visited with three either sitting or later to be elected Roman Catholic popes. His credentials for commenting on the nature and future of religion are impressive but obviously not infallible. It may be a bit of a stretch to put him alongside the other figures who think of religion in terms of improving personal orientations, but it seems his thinking fits better here than anywhere else.

In *The Future of Faith* Cox suggests that there is an unanticipated resurgence of religion going on that runs counter to the view that religion is dying but also counter to many traditional assumptions about how religion functions—especially as a corporate structure. This resurgence stresses the horizontal rather than the vertical nature of spiritual experience—or to use technical terminology, it emphasizes immanence rather than transcendence. This approach, which relies on the pragmatic and experiential aspects of faith as a way of living, displaces the creedal and institutional aspects. The popular or non-scholarly expression of this trend is expressed by the increasing number of people who say they are "spiritual but not religious."

To elaborate on his contention that this is (or should be) what is happening Cox divides Christian history into three periods. The first period, which lasted from the experiential encounter with Jesus through the period in which Christianity was a small, persecuted minority, he calls "The Age of Faith." The second period, which began as Christianity became more and more accepted in the Roman culture and was eventually afforded privileged status, was marked by the development of creeds and a hierarchical clergy. During this period a religion about Jesus replaced loyalty to Jesus, and the church became institutionalized. Cox calls this "The Age of Belief" and argues that it has lasted a long time and is only now beginning to be questioned.

Cox contends that we are on the threshold of a third age— "The Age of the Spirit." To be sure, some aspects of this way of being a Christian were present in the thought and life of Christian mystics in the past, but now the orientation is becoming more widespread. The new development will put far more emphasis on the role of the Holy Spirit in the Christian life, as do Pentecostal movements (which are experiencing rapid growth.) Admittedly, the term "spirit" can stand for several things: navel gazing, for instance; or disciplined practice bordering on legalism, or openness to the secular dimensions of life as well as the sacred. Cox would put stress on the term as denoting the experiential rather than the creedal as the most valuable aspect of being faithful.

Cox suggests that this new perspective offers three kinds of appeal: 1) it is a way of protesting against propositional orthodoxy; 2) it attempts to give expression to awe and wonder; and 3) it is porous to other faiths. The Age of the Spirit will have some similarities to the Age of Faith that was characteristic of the early church. The vision Cox sets forth is summarized as follows:

> I have shown how Christianity, which began as a movement of Spirit guided by faith, soon clotted into a catalog of beliefs administered by a clerical class. But now, due to a number of different factors, the process is being reversed. Faith is resurgent, while dogma is dying. The spiritual, communal, and justice-seeking dimensions of Christianity are now its leading edge as the twenty-first century hurtles forward, and this change is taking place along with similar reformations in the other world religions.[4]

In some of the chapters Cox deals with the church fathers, as does Thomas Oden, but draws very different lessons from reading them. Oden sees the period of the church fathers as the source of orthodoxy; Cox sees it as a time of diversity that was unfortunately foreclosed by the institutionalizing of Christianity. That two highly competent scholars should read the same history differently illustrates how in dealing with religious outlooks much depends upon how evidence is interpreted and used to substantiate a controlling perspective.

---

4. Cox, *The Future of Faith*, 213.

To embrace faith with only minimal institutional involvement is to put the emphasis upon the individual and the benefits the individual derives from being religious. Clearly there is a major difference between how Cox advocates doing this and how many of those discussed earlier in the chapter do so. Cox shares the concern for social justice shared by persons of good will; many televangelists do not. Cox would be critical of huge institutional structures that replace the traditional forms of ecclesiastical practice with innovative alternatives pandering to an infatuation with the gaudy and the novel; few television preachers or mega-church pastors would be. Cox is open to persons of other traditions whose reliance on faith is differently expressed; many exponents of Christian self-help are not. But these significant differences do not wipe out a shared tendency to understand the function of religious conviction to be an instrument of personal well-being.

An Unexpected Example

In *Religion for Atheists: A Nonbelievers Guide to the Uses of Religion*, Alan de Botton, a Swiss architect as well as a writer and philosopher, contends that religion offers several benefits that are much needed by modern people and can be had without holding particular beliefs about the supernatural. Botton argues that even atheists should support religion as a way of making life better. Religion can be valuable because it promotes morality, inspires travel, trains minds, and encourages gratitude for the beauty of life. Some of the benefits to which Botton points are corporate rather than merely individual in nature, but his view that religion is valuable for its contribution to human well-being has much in common with the other approaches described in the chapter. To suggest that religion plays a beneficial role in human affairs and is useful, even if it is mistaken in its beliefs, can reduce it to a tool humans manipulate rather than a response to a Reality that makes a claim upon them.

To embrace religion for the benefits it offers to the human condition without coupling that anticipation with the trusting surrender to One who makes a claim upon us may be to misunderstand

Seeking Personal Well-Being

the gospel. To the extent the preachers of well-being either do that themselves, or are responded to by people who do, they may not be the gurus we need. According to the Bible the benefits of Christian discipleship are not to be had without something like repentance, and that comfort is not to be obtained by what might be called spiritual management on no-risk terms. To recognize the holiness of God and to give oneself to the service of the Ultimate involves a surrender of the self as the precondition of fulfillment. It is not clear that an emphasis on the value of religion as a source of well-being understands this to be the case.

To be sure, there are differences between the various proponents of using religion for its benefits as to what they take to be a healthy and desirable human condition. Their views as to the nature of spiritual fulfillment are not the same. Self-aggrandizing prosperity doesn't fit with a view of communal interaction that is mutually helpful and supportive. Nor is faith rightly understood or practiced on a purely private basis.

It may be that some of the approaches we have described in this chapter represent the same suspicion or rejection of institutions as the Tea Party does in the political realm. They place emphasis on the personal and individual capacity to change, improve, or advance human well-being—though some, especially Warren and Botton, do point out the place for community support in doing this. Many of them indicate we must repudiate the past in order to allow a new era to emerge. It is easier to demonstrate what has been inadequate in the past than to provide assurance that the new order will be more promising. For all the problems associated with institutional religion what would society today be like had previous generations not created it? Cox appreciatively reports on his visits with the popes, but without the developments Cox decries they would not have been available for him to visit. Cox knows this and indicates why he thinks the papacy is important—but he does not fully recognize how dependent the papacy is on a more structural orientation to Christianity.

Then, too, we need to ask whether the present enthusiasm for the spiritual in contrast with the religious will prove to have a long, sustaining future. Will it yield the hoped-for results or will it evaporate when the shortcomings and frustrations that attend much human existence catch up with it—as they often do even with carefully orchestrated idealistic agendas? It is easy to commend the imagined benefits of the still unknown future and compare them with the known shortcomings of the past—but is doing so realistic? To raise this question is to encourage the search for the better path, to be open rather than closed, to be realistic yet not cynical. To ignore or to underplay the reality of human tendencies to malfeasance and corruption, or to suppose that only the benighted generations of the past or the officialdoms of the present are prone to them may be a type of self delusion.

The classic study of how well-intentioned people who are confident of their righteousness can be cruelly protective is found in Dostoevsky's *The Grand Inquisitor*. Dostoevsky astutely portrays how those who believe they espouse the truth are tempted to control the destiny of others for the benefit of those others. Can we be confident that being supposedly spiritual rather than religious will necessarily guarantees immunity from that kind of behavior? Can inquisitors wear t-shirts and jeans as well as cassocks and Geneva gowns? Does any religious outlook guarantee immunity from misuse?

THREE

Approaches Involving Group Identities

All of the approaches discussed in this chapter are related to group identities. That may seem strange to any who that have heard the quotation from Alfred North Whitehead that "Religion is what man does with his solitariness." But there is an important relationship between religion and group experience even though that relationship can be expressed in different ways. One of the ways religion functions to shape group identity is to prompt the formation of communities of special outlooks and behavior. These communities often follow special rules for living in order to achieve some moral and spiritual uniqueness. But, in contrast, religion is often influenced and even shaped by group experiences—or by particular group experiences. In this case religion becomes a reflection of some group perspective to which it attributes special significance. This means that approaches involving group identity can take two forms, even though in both cases a distinct relationship between religion and group behavior provides the clue for understanding the nature and future of Christianity.

Christian Church Separatism in the Past

The early Christians were, in the eyes of many interpreters, a group identified by their distinctive beliefs and behavior, which stood in

The Nature and Future of Christianity

contrast to those of the surrounding culture. When the church was recognized as the official religion of the Roman Empire it adapted itself to the prevailing culture and lost the distinctive qualities that characterized it as movement. As this happened some Christians felt called to a vocation characterized by an intentionally different way of living. At first this special behavior was pursued mainly by individuals, but before too long it became a group phenomenon and monastic communities were formed and incorporated into the wider church as a special witness. Ever since, Christianity has struggled with the tension between the need to adapt to the culture in order to function effectively within it and the impulse to maintain itself as a community identified by special practices. Many Christians believe it is possible for Christianity as a whole to go back to being like the early church—an endeavor of the whole body of believers to be clearly distinctive. But others doubt that is either possible or necessary, and they believe that behavioral uniqueness is possible only in special or minority groups. These groups may be officially connected to the main body of believers, as are most monastic orders, or they may seek to achieve minority uniqueness, in which case they are usually designated separatists.

The spiritual dynamic characterizing such groups is almost always opposite to that of the prosperity gospel. Self limitation, even self effacement, replaces self-aggrandizement as the governing principle. This draws on a different strain in the Bible—probably a far more dominant one—than the prosperity gospel, and there is no question this is a compelling vocation for some individuals. Attempts to develop a unique group life embodying Christian ideals are many and varied. Not only have they taken the form of church-related monasticism, but also of separatist lifestyles such as those of the Shakers, who devised their own unique pattern of living. Nor were the Shakers the only eighteenth-century group to embody the separatist impulse. The Ephrata community in Pennsylvania once flourished as an example of separatist uniqueness. The Oneida community in New York state and the Amana community in Iowa followed later, but they no longer have separatist qualities. The achievements of such communities are often admired, even by those who do not follow their calling. For instance, many monastic

Approaches Involving Group Identities

orders provide charitable or educational services that are greatly appreciated. They may even make special wines that people consume with pleasure. The buildings the Shaker communities erected are now used for museums and schools and are remarkable for their architectural magnificence. The furniture the Shakers created is still cherished for its simplicity of design by those fortunate or affluent enough to own it.

Some of these communities were too small to remain alive indefinitely; others may have died out because their practices could not be sustained. Such communities, especially those celibate like the Shakers, have to attract members from outside themselves in order to continue existing, or otherwise they die. Moreover, any group has to handle money and property in order to survive, and if it will not do so it can carry on only by connecting to a wider church that does that for them. Separatist groups that manage to survive may do so by being more prudent in their stringency than those that lose out. For instance, while the Amish can be considered a separatist movement somewhat like the Shakers, they have survived not least because they are not celibate and because they permit individual ownership of property and the management of money, and they have their own versions of productive work. That makes a difference.

A number of separatist groups are still functioning; others are developing in response to a continuing vocation on the part of some to live in a special sort of way. Both claim to offer a model for Christianity's future. These can be arranged along a spectrum starting with traditional monasticism (which is still practiced, mainly in Roman Catholic and Anglican traditions) and moving toward examples of groups with far more limited versions of special identity. It is impossible to understand the present nature of Christianity without being aware of the extent to which such groups exist and seek to understand the gospel as a calling to live according to alterative expectations.

The Nature and Future of Christianity

Contemporary Intentional Communities

Perhaps the best-known example of a contemporary approach to Christianity that centers on group identity is the Taizé community, based in France but known and respected in a much larger part of the world. It shares some features of traditional monasticism but has developed some of it own special practices. This is a community of about one hundred brothers who have Protestant, Eastern Orthodox, and the Roman Catholic backgrounds. They come from some thirty countries around the world and are devoted to peace and justice through prayer and meditation. Taizé was founded in 1940 by a Protestant, Roger Schutz, who has authored several books on the contemplative life and its relationship to social outreach. Over a hundred thousand pilgrims, mostly young people, make pilgrimages to Taizé community every year, where they engage for various lengths of time in Bible study, sharing, and communal work. These pilgrims are attracted to the movement, but not many of them become fully committed to it. The community has developed worship materials that are widely used elsewhere, even by churches that pay little attention to all the practices of the Taizé movement.

Brother Roger Schutz has from his very youth bridged the gap between Catholic and Protestant spirituality. At thirteen he went through a period as an agnostic—occasioned by an initial encounter with the Darwinian explanation of natural history. He then encountered the thought of Pascal and underwent a bout of tuberculosis. He undertook theological studies with the intention of using it to better understand literature, but when his sister was remarkably healed of a illness associated with pregnancy, he returned to his theological studies with a sense that it might be important for guiding lifestyle choices. Early on he was elected president, over his protests, of the Student Christian Association in Europe, and the trials of the Second World War closed in upon him. He searched for a place to live in a special way and found a location near to persons in great need.

When he occupied a rundown house in eastern France in the early 1940s he found himself opening its doors to needy refugees and cultivating the land in order to provide life's necessities. He was harassed by the Gestapo and was driven from the house. He then went to Geneva where he pursued further theological studies and wrote a dissertation on monasticism as a form of spirituality. While in Geneva he was joined by two others, and then all three eventually returned to Taizé where they were viewed with suspicion because they were pursuing a monastic lifestyle even though they were Protestants and had no official ecclesiastical endorsement. A Roman Catholic joined the group after which they were granted the use of the largely unused local Roman Catholic Church for prayer and worship by Pope John XXIII. Later the community built its own church. Each member remained officially committed to the tradition of his origin. The group practiced a common life from the beginning, but only later did Brother Roger write the *Rule of Taizé*, which has subsequently been the governing document of the community.

The practices that have developed from those early events are recognized and often admired by many people all around the world. There are many ways in which Taizé transforms traditional creedal and institutional religion, but it does so in a communal rather than individualistic way. It promotes the renewal and extension of religious practice—not its repudiation. To be sure, it is still a minority movement, but one that extends and enhances the tradition rather than eclipsing or repudiating it.

A second example of the communal pattern is the Iona Community in Scotland, which may not be quite as well known as Taizé and is less neo-monastic. Iona was founded in 1938 by a Presbyterian, George Macleod. In 2009 it had 270 full members, about 1,800 associates, and some 1,600 friends. They come from many denominations and countries. They spend some time in one of three residential centers, the chief of which is on the island of Iona, off the coast of Scotland. There they engage in rebuilding an ancient abbey as well as engaging in study and common worship. In the winter they devote themselves to social service work in urban areas. Their liturgical and study materials are published under a "Wild Goose" imprint and are used by many beyond the group itself.

The Nature and Future of Christianity

The Iona Community has many similarities to the Taizé Community. It reaches out to young people from many nations, hosts those wishing to make spiritual pilgrimages, and plays an active role in the quest for social justice. However, its small core membership is not committed to celibacy, and it is less closely affiliated with Roman Catholic leadership even though some of its members belong to that church.

Although historical monastic communities related to the Roman Catholic Church seem to have a steady existence, efforts to establish other kinds of separatist communities in America have not attained the size, strength or vigor of Taizé and Iona. Pendle Hill, a Quaker center near Philadelphia, might be mentioned, but it operates more as a learning center than as a neo-monastic community. Koinonia Farm in Georgia also embodies the impulse to live in New Testament patterns but with more emphasis on farming than on study. There is a conference ground in eastern Pennsylvania called Kirkridge that has never attained quite the notoriety of Taizé or Iona but pursues the same objectives. It may be that the American efforts have lacked the unique leadership that was offered by Brother Schutz and George Macleod. Neither of the American efforts were marked by any of the interest in Catholic spirituality that was present in Taizé and to a lesser extent in Iona. It may be that the American attempts were simply too Protestant to sustain such a communal spirituality. Or it may be that American culture as a whole is simply so obsessed with a worldly concept of success that it enables mega-churches oriented on a prosperity gospel to thrive, whereas something like a Taizé or an Iona simply doesn't flower. Whatever is the reason the matter is worth contemplating.

Merely to create small separatist groups does not guarantee authentic allegiance to the Christian ideal. The agenda can go bizarre, as it did, for instance, in the case of the Branch Davidians, the group in Texas that was raided by the FBI and Drug Enforcement Agency several years ago. Although this group had a communal lifestyle, the arbitrary authoritarianism of its leader created problems that eventually brought about tragedy. Moreover, its activities were far less transparent than is true of Taizé and Iona, which, like traditional Roman Catholic monasticism, conduct their affairs with openness. Everything they do is open to public scrutiny and people are welcome to observe what is being done. The Davidians stand as a sober reminder that religious groups are not immune from misuse.

Intentionalism without a Geographical Center

Unlike Taizé and Iona, many other groups that seek to achieve a special level of devotional uniqueness do not have a geographical center providing them with a place that gives them a special identity, but they work within the structures of the institutional church as special groups for the purpose of revitalizing Christian commitment and practice. For instance, the *Opus Dei* movement in the Roman Catholic Church utilizes special group identity as a means of making faith more meaningful and devotional life more disciplined. This group, with members scattered in many congregations in over ninety countries, is estimated to have had over ninety thousand members in the year 2010. Composed largely, but not entirely of laypersons, this organization calls its members to observe special practices of holiness within the framework of ordinary life. It was founded in 1928 by José Maria Escriva, recognized by Pope John Paul XII in 1950 and given the special status of a personal prelature, which means its head exercises the supervisory role of a bishop, thus bypassing (so to speak) the authority of the local bishop of the dioceses in which the various members live. The practices and influence of this movement were highlighted somewhat unsympathetically in Dan Brown's novel, *The Da Vinci Code*.

Opus Dei is controversial in part because it operates somewhat secretly, and because it is dedicated to the defense and reinforcement of a conservative Roman Catholicism. It represents a counter thrust against the Second Vatican Council's trend towards *aggiornamento*, or updating the stance of the church. Therefore, unlike Taizé and Iona, it is not ecumenical in either spirit or intention. Members of this movement commit themselves to prescribed spiritual obligations, a monetary discipline, and even to a form of flagellation that involves wearing an uncomfortable device on the thigh for up to two hours per day. This is a recast version of the monastic impulse that suggests the ongoing appeal of the ascetic ideal, even if adapted to ordinary living in the contemporary world.

Another movement that has arisen within the Roman Catholic Church but now has many followers in the Episcopal Church bears the short name *Cursillo*. The longer Spanish designation, *Cursillos de Cristianidad*, means "short course in Christianity." This movement gathers together a small group of church members, usually from one parish, and makes a three-day weekend retreat for an intensive course in basic Christian teaching. According to many reports the regimen is strictly prescribed and dutifully adhered to, and open-ended searching about matters of faith is discouraged.

This experience, which was offered only in Spanish when it was first started, has been introduced into all 160 dioceses of the Episcopal Church in the United States, though this does not mean every parish has participated. Although the main focus is on learning doctrine, this is accompanied by attention to spiritual development and the creation of leadership for what is called "the fourth day," that is, life back in the parish setting following a three-day weekend retreat. This process has the intention of overcoming the theological illiteracy of most local congregations, but it also has the danger of creating a group that imagines itself to be uniquely endowed with attitudes and insights lacking in those who have not participated in the program—resulting in an imagined spiritual elitism that can have divisive consequences.

Defining Christianity from Group Identity

In contrast to using the gospel for guidance in the formation of special group identities others use group identities as the basis for understanding the gospel. The clearest examples of this are liberation theologies. The term is almost always attached to a group that can be identified as oppressed and asserting its right to be released

Approaches Involving Group Identities

from that condition. Sometimes the term "liberation" is omitted and we hear about "Black Theology," "Feminist or Womanist Theology," or "LGBTQ Theology." Each of these ways of thinking about religious matters contends that the experience of a particular group offers a unique position from which to be involved in the religious enterprise.

This is clear in two quotations from James Cone, the author of *A Black Theology of Liberation*.

> Black Theology believes that the black community itself is precisely where Christ is at work. The Christ event in twentieth century America is a black event, that is, an event of liberation taking place in the black community in which black people recognize that it is incumbent upon them to throw off the claims of white oppression by whatever means they regard as suitable.[1]

> The revolutionary situation forces Black Theology to shun all abstract principles dealing with what is the "right" and "wrong" course of action. There is only one principle which guides the thinking of Black Theology: an unqualified commitment to the black community as that community seeks to define its existence in light of God's liberating action in the world.[2]

To those who find this startling and contrary to the whole attempt of much modern Christianity to become inclusive Cone contends that white theology is just as much a product of a particular community as Black Theology is. White theology is discredited because it has accepted and sometimes even furthered the oppression of black people. It therefore stands under judgment and is to be repudiated.

Other versions of liberation theology use the identity of a special group as the key to interpreting the Christian message. Gustavo Gutierrez, author of *A Theology of Liberation*, contends that groups engaged in the struggle for justice in places like South America understand the human situation quite differently than Western

---

1. Cone, *A Black Theology of Liberation*, 24.
2. Ibid., 33.

The Nature and Future of Christianity

Christianity has frequently done with its identification with domineering power. This new reasoning emphasizes praxis—that is, inspired action and reflection instead of principles—and focuses on the struggle for justice as the work of the oppressed, for whom God has a preferential option. The struggle for justice becomes itself a salvific work. Gutierrez contrasts his way of thinking to the traditional view.

> The very radicalness and totality of the salvific process requires this relationship [to the oppressed]. Nothing escapes this process, nothing is outside the pale of the action of Christ and the gift of the Spirit. This gives human history its profound unity. Those who reduce the work of salvation are indeed those who limit it to the strictly "religious" sphere and are not aware of the universality of the process. It is those who think that the work of Christ touches the social order in which we live only indirectly or tangentially, and not in its roots and basic structure. It is those who in order to protect salvation (or to protect their own interests) lift salvation from the midst of history, where men and social classes struggle to liberate themselves from the slavery and oppression to which other men and social classes have subjected them. It is those who refuse to see that the salvation of Christ is a radical liberation from all misery, all despotism, all alienation. It is those who by trying to "save" the work of Christ will "lose" it.[3]

Feminist or womanist theology is yet another example of the way group identity is used to understand the nature of the Christian message in new ways. This has had a significant impact on Christian thinking in the last four decades even though it is expressed in a variety of ways. Perhaps the most extreme example of this is found in the thought of Mary Daly, who taught for years at Boston College, a Roman Catholic institution. Daly achieved notoriety at one time for her refusal to have any men in her classes. In her early thinking she entertained the idea that Christianity could be transformed from inside to become more open to the concerns of women. But in 1971

---

3. Gutierrez, *A Theology of Liberation*, 177f.

Approaches Involving Group Identities

she was invited to preach at the Memorial Church at Harvard and declared that Christianity cannot be rendered compatible with the experience of women, and urged its total repudiation. Almost all the women who were present showed their support, as did a few men.

At the other end of the spectrum there are feminists who believe Christianity can be rendered more open to women and that as that happens it will become more open, tolerant, and nurturing to all. According to those who espouse this view, the nurturing traits associated with women will overcome hierarchy and disciplinary postures typical of males and give church life a new set of appealing features. The term "womanist theology" is sometimes used to describe this position, but the term is also frequently associated with several thinkers who link Black liberation with feminist liberations.

Somewhere along the line between these outer points are women who develop theology from their identity but speak of "partnership"—a term use by Professor Letty Russell of Yale. Her outlook regards diversity as an important value. The freedom for which women yearn, Russell argues, is a freedom to be able to serve others but not to be subservient to them. It includes pursuing God's intention of justice, freedom, and peace for all humanity, the pursuit of which may be especially dependent on the sensitivities of women in shaping Christianity. The differences between these various expressions of women's concerns are probably less important than the similarities between them as approaches that stem from a group identity.

Still another example that indicates how religious thought and practice can be derived from group identity is LGBTQ Theology. This has been the most recent of the outlooks to have risen from group experience, but that does not make it any less important. The identities involved are possibly somewhat more diverse, and the numbers smaller. Moreover, the issues raised are more highly charged in the present state of our cultural warfare.

The Nature and Future of Christianity

All four of these approaches are associated with a revisionist reading of history. For instance, feminists have helped us to see what crucial roles women played in the early Christian movement, and a major work by the Yale historian John Boswell has argued that up until the twelfth century the Christian church was fairly open toward homosexuality. Moreover, pressure from women has led to the use of inclusive language in much contemporary worship. Many congregations now have women as heads of the pastoral staff, and seminaries have significant percentages of women in their student bodies and on the faculty.

The appeal of these various liberation theologies to members of the groups out of which they emerge is very great, and there is no question that the idea of being freed from oppression has a major role in the biblical story. But this does not evaporate all the problems. When more than one group claims its experience is the clue to religious identity then conflicts arise. Sympathetic individuals and institutions seeking to be fair may have to make choices as to which claims to prioritize. This may not satisfy all the groups.

Moreover, doing theology in this way involves a momentous reversal of some assumptions that have long held that universalizable and inclusive ideas are more valuable than particularistic ones. The presumption in favor of openness to all on an equal basis is quite important in Enlightenment thinking and in theologies built upon that thinking. Such thinking finds itself radically challenged by new group-oriented particularism. This tension is not unknown even within the liberation theologies we have mentioned. Remember those quotations from Professor Cone cited earlier, those declaring that Black experience is the only way to Christian understanding? They have to be read in conjunction with some of his later thinking. For instance, in the preface to a documentary history of Black Theology he helped co-edit he writes:

> We Black theologians should not only be prepared to answer what a certain segment of the Black community thinks about the ultimate, but also the question, "What is the truth as applied to humanity?" I do not believe that we should limit our analysis of the truth to a certain ethnic manifestation of it in the Black community. This means

Approaches Involving Group Identities

that our development of a Black Theology must start from the particularity of the Black experience but cannot be limited to it. Therefore, we should create a perspective on Black Theology that invites other oppressed people to share with us in the search for the truth that defines us all. We must not allow Black Theology to reduce itself to an ethnic particularism.[4]

Do oppressed groups in their several forms constitute a special condition that offers a unique and perhaps only basis for understanding the gospel? If so, how do their understandings relate to one another and how can they be brought together in a more holistic gestalt? That issue is still before us, and may well be the focus of debates for quite some time to come.

---

4. Cone and Wilmore, *Black Theology*, 619f.

FOUR

Religious Concern for Society

Among the many options for thinking about the role and future of Christianity one of the most important is concern about the health and viability of society. Despite historical evidence that Christianity has sometimes been intermeshed with oppression and exploitation, it is now generally assumed that Christian social witness favors the creation of a more just and peaceful social order, one in which justice is understood as a matter of beneficence and harsh and insensitive practices have been overcome. But we are currently in the midst of intense and divisive disagreements about the proper nature of Christian witness to and responsibility for the world. The rise of a different kind of concern for society that has come from the religious right challenges the assumption that a socially concerned Christianity will always have a liberal, neighbor-supporting, justice-oriented, and peace-endorsing quality.

The Rise of Christian Social Concern

The current debates as to the proper role of Christianity in relationship to society have historical roots that go back a long way. At the beginning Christians were a struggling and even despised minority and therefore were in no position to relate to society through its political and economic structures. Then, when Constantine

The Nature and Future of Christianity

recognized Christianity as a tolerated religion and later Theodosius I made it the official religion of the Roman Empire, Christians found themselves with access to positions of power and influence that the majority of them felt obligated to use in order to uphold a stable social order. As a result most Christians have participated directly in much of Western society and long since have abandoned such early practices as the refusal to exercise secular office, to engage in military service, or to lend money at interest. Both Catholicism and Protestantism have presumed there are advantages to exercising influence and even control over public life and have learned to overlook the fact that the moral ideals of the gospel are incompatible with many of the political and economic functions of society in any of its prevalent manifestations.

The early twentieth century saw the development of vigorous efforts to bring social practices in line with Christian ideals. The American economic system at the end of the nineteenth and beginning of the twentieth century was marked by glaring differences in its rewards to individuals, a lack of any public programs for persons suffering misfortune, and horrific uses of naked power to keep labor in a subservient role. A Baptist preacher, Walter Rauschenbusch, was disturbed by the conditions of the poor and downtrodden he observed in Hell's kitchen in New York. By challenging the use of the term "gospel" to speak only of theological ideas having to do with personal salvation he called upon Christians to work for a more just society. His call for social change involved not only economic fairness but the reduction of international conflict.

Two of Rauschenbusch's books played pivotal roles in advancing his influence. One, published in 1907 with the title *Christianity and the Social Crisis*, calls attention to the intolerable conditions under which great numbers of Americans live and indicts Christianity for its complicity in that state of affairs. The other, *A Theology for the Social Gospel*, which appeared ten years later, provides a more systematic defense of the Christian mandate to alleviate poverty, overcome injustice, and bring the principalities and powers of this world under scrutiny and judgment. Rauschenbusch was convinced that what he called "a social movement" was afoot and that "for the first time in history the spirit of Christianity has had a

Religious Concern for Society

chance to form a working partnership with real social and psychological science."[1] He believed that the door was open for religion to benefit from the "historic advent of democracy." The apparent optimism of those remarks is tempered by the rigor with which Rauschenbusch analyzed the power of sin in the social dynamics of his day, but nevertheless Rauschenbusch's thinking did much to push Christian social concern in idealistic directions.

Although the role of Rauschenbusch in articulating this new perspective had unique importance he was not alone. On December 4, 1908, the Federal Council of Churches adopted a document calling for Christians to concern themselves with the alleviation of many social wrongs. It called for equal rights for those in all stations of life; for the right of labor to organize; for conciliation and arbitration in labor disputes; for the abolition of child labor; for regulations to improve working conditions—especially those of women; for lowering the hours of labor and abolishing the sweat-shop; for release from employment one day of seven; for a minimum living wage; and for the provision of old age benefits. By adopting the social creed ecumenical mainline Christianity found itself coming squarely into conflict with those—often some of its own members—who defended a completely private enterprise system. The very same conservatives who opposed Darwin's idea of evolution were often, without recognizing it, supporting a social system based on the premises of Social Darwinism.

While this Creed highlighted the moral problems in the industrial system, socially concerned Christians subsequently came to recognize two other major features of society that were difficult to reconcile with the gospel. Over time, more and more Christians realized that racial segregation in the South and racial prejudice in the North (both manifestations of "racism") were morally wrong. In addition, many Christians—disillusioned with the outcome of the First World War, a war that was supposedly fought to make the world safe for democracy—embraced a pacifist ethic, even in churches that did not have that as part of their heritage. This trend was spurred on when it was discovered that many of the reports

---

1. Rauschenbusch, *A Theology for the Social Gospel*, 5.

of atrocities attributed to the enemy were untrue. Preachers and others made pledges never again to engage in military action. Of these two agendas, both of which extended the scope of the social creed, criticism of racial segregation and injustice was probably more widely embraced than pacifism, but both became prominent features of socially concerned Christianity by the middle of the twentieth century, along with continuing—but perhaps slightly diminished—attention to economic justice.

The Social Gospel was associated with what was then generally called theological modernism; that is, a version of Christian faith congenial to the Enlightenment. The correlation was not complete but it was undeniable. One aspect of the Enlightenment that gave the Social Gospel both identity and impulse was a confidence in the ability of human beings to achieve social transformations on the basis of moral resolve. Many saw such commitments to be the outgrowth of religious faith, but others pointed out that they could be made without the necessary backing of traditionally orthodox beliefs. That latter view reached its clearest expression in the Ethical Culture Movement, which attracted the allegiance of persons from several religious backgrounds by "bracketing out overbeliefs." Moral idealism functioned as a kind of common faith whose capacity to warrant commitment was believed to be something around which all could rally.

The Conservative Response

For years the response of theological and political conservatives to these social stands was to deny they were legitimate concerns of the church. Conservatives called for keeping the churches out of business and politics. In earlier periods this reticence was motivated by the desire to keep the Christian community from being divided over what were considered political positions having divisive consequences. For instance, long before the controversy created by the Social Gospel, the ante-bellum southern Presbyterian Church developed a doctrine of the spirituality of the church that enabled it to remain aloof from the struggle for abolition in the nineteenth century with its inevitable divisiveness. But when the spokesmen for the Social Gospel indicted social conditions they regarded as evil, every major mainline denomination was affected by rising controversy between social conservatives and advocates of a socially relevant Christianity, often with divisive consequences for many mainline denominations.

Social Christianity has undergone many changes since its appearance a century ago. The heady days of Christian idealism are now ancient and possibly irretrievable. One change came about when the rise of totalitarian regimes in Europe threatened to overrun Western democratic societies and prompted many to reconsider the adequacy of a pacifist stance. Reinhold Niebuhr is usually regarded as the central figure in challenging the relevance of idealistic pacifism—even though in his early years he was associated with a more political type of pacifism. In his years as a pastor in Detroit he observed the harsh injustices of an economic system unchecked by social controls and the countervailing power of organized labor. Later, coming as he did to judge the threats in Europe so serious as to require military resistance, he embraced a Christian realism informed by the Augustinian premise that we have to live in two different social constructs—the City of God where loving relationships are possible, and the City of this World, where the use of coercive political power is the main thing that guarantees order in society.

Niebuhr became influential in shaping American policy—a public theologian probably without equal in the contemporary scene. He was vigorously criticized by those, both religious and secular, still wedded to social idealism as well as by those who benefitted from the social injustices he deplored. Interestingly enough, Niebuhr's version of Christianity is a form of theological liberalism, but is characterized by a hard-nosed rather than sanguine view of human nature and its constructs. With respect to economic matters and racial justice his views were consistent with aims of the Social Gospel but he was more aware of the kind of resistance to social justice likely to be mounted by the privileged sectors of society than were many advocates of the Social Gospel.

The Nature and Future of Christianity

The other major development that has altered the dynamics of religious concern for society has occurred more recently. Very different from Niebuhr's challenge, it has nevertheless altered the dynamic of Christianity in America. In 1976 Jerry Falwell, the Baptist pastor of a huge church in Lynchburg, Virginia, decided that the strategy of combating liberal Christian concern for society by insisting that such concern has no place in the church was mistaken. He conducted a series of rallies to solicit public activism on behalf of the conservative moral values he considered important for a healthy social order. This led to the creation of the Moral Majority three years later.

The agenda of this group was also an effort to implement Christian values in the public sphere but the values it advocated were quite different. Although the Moral Majority as a movement has since been dissolved, the right wing religious activism it created is still very much alive. The values it stands for are now strongly endorsed and vehemently supported by a political outlook that has achieved enormous influence, particularly in the conservative side of the Republican Party. The social stands advocated by this movement include support for traditional family patterns (and opposition to same sex marriage), support for the use of military power to deal with threats such as terrorism, opposition to abortion and even to Planned Parenthood, and the unqualified approval of profit-making as a form of stewardship. This kind of social concern flows out of a very different reading of Christian moral imperatives than that put forth by the Social Gospel. Today, the so-called "culture wars" that are present in political life are felt in the churches as much as they are felt in the wider culture. Although the new religious right favors so-called personal values it strongly aims to support those values by public means.

These disagreements about the social imperatives of the gospel often exist between individual members of the same religious body and not merely between so-called liberal groups and so-called conservative groups. Church leaders are often more liberal than the rank and file of their members, and in some cases more conservative. In the case of Roman Catholicism, for instance, where the teaching of the bishops on matters of corporate and economic behavior is closer to those of the Social Gospel than to those of the political right, conservative politicians who staunchly defend the church's opposition to abortion and birth control simply ignore the matters with which they disagree with the bishops. Meanwhile many working Catholics who are sympathetic to the economics outlook of the bishops quietly ignore their teaching about reproductive matters. This selective taking of exceptions to the teaching authority of the Catholic bishops is no more decisive in determining the social outlooks of the rank and file of Roman Catholics than the extent to which many Protestant constituencies disagree with their leaders as to what constitutes morally commendable public policy. To put it bluntly, the effectiveness of the churches as instruments of social transformation has been losing ground precisely because many churches are as divided about the issues as is the society. It may not be possible to avoid this fate in a society where religious allegiance is purely voluntary.

New Forms of Social Concern

One response to this situation is to call for a resurgent social Christianity. To be sure, social concern as it took place a century ago may not be easily applied to the very complex situation of our day. However, some of the same impulses can be important even though they are now expressed in different ways. The political and economic realities of our time may not be as different from what they were in the late nineteenth and early twentieth century as is sometimes supposed. Then, the affluent rolled tobacco in hundred dollar bills to show off their economic standing; today they badger boards of directors into offering seven and eight figure compensation packages while paying employees minimum wages that are insufficient to support a decent standard of living.

Thinking about the economic aspect of the social process now involves concern for justice not merely in the industrial sphere where people toil for a living, but also concern for justice and responsibility in the so-called financial sphere, where gain is obtained by cleverness rather than by sweat. Discontent with conditions in

The Nature and Future of Christianity

this sphere is now substantial and growing—as the Occupy Wall Street movement has been demonstrating. But rather than merely hype the discontent, more attention needs to be given to what would constitute sober, reliable, and prudent standards for behavior in this kind of entrepreneurial endeavor. Too little thought is being given to this, and the tentative and fragmentary efforts that are being mounted enjoy little consensus or informed treatment from the average pulpit. The challenges we face in thinking about this matter are enormous, and progress is stymied by polarized thinking among the religiously concerned just as much as it is stalemated by deadlocks within both legislative and judicial branches of government.

In observance of the hundredth anniversary of the Social Creed of the Churches a number of ecclesiastical leaders have drawn up a Social Creed for the twenty-first century.[2] This new version builds on the concern of the older creed for economic justice by identifying new forms of injustice that need to be condemned on moral grounds—such as forced labor, human trafficking, and wages that do not provide for adequate family support. It calls for a rehabilitative rather than vindictive approach to criminal justice—one that aims to restore wrongdoers to a place in society rather than stress the punitive functions of criminal law. It opposes the death penalty.

In setting forth a concept of civil life compatible with Christian ideals this new Creed calls for policies that benefit the most vulnerable members of society, for high-quality public education available to all, for budget policies that reduce the disparities between the rich and the poor, for just immigration policies, for social efforts to help sustain family life, and for putting emphasis on the importance of public service as a vocation.

The final section of this New Creed stresses the importance of both environmental concerns and peacemaking. It commends simpler lifestyles, urges concern for clear air, clean water, and healthy food produced in ways that care for the land as a sustainable resource. It stresses the importance of global trade.

---

2. National Council of Churches. *A Social Creed for the 21st Century*. http://www.ncccusa.org/news/ga2007.socialcreed.html.

Religious Concern for Society

An important and crucial emerging focus of concern has the name "peacemaking." This is a recasting of much thinking about the problem of violence. It differs both from the pacifism of the type associated with the Social Gospel and from the outlook of the realist critics. Instead of being primarily concerned as to whether or not the use of military action is permissible for Christians loyal to the New Testament heritage or needed to bring about justice, it directs attention to overcoming the causes of potential conflicts and thus prevents them from igniting into massive warfare. Peacemaking involves, not merely making a judgment about the moral legitimacy or illegitimacy of using military means, which are developing staggering capacities for the infliction of destruction, but also paying attention to the causes of conflict and how they can be lessened or eliminated before hostilities break out. It is becoming as much a focus of academic interest as environmental studies, sometimes in institutions where one would not expect to find it embraced.

The other major area to which contemporary thinking is directing Christian social attention is concern about the care of the earth. For a good deal of Christian history, and particularly with the development of modern technology, it has been assumed that nature was created to be utilized for human betterment. The Genesis story of creation can plausibly be read to reinforce that view. As a consequence, human beings have developed many ways of using the resources of nature to support increasingly comfortable yet environmentally depleting ways of living. The dire consequences of doing this indefinitely, which scientists are now calling to our attention, are sobering. The threats of an environmental catastrophe stem from excessive pollution, the use of nonrenewable resources with abandon, and burning carbon fuels that are responsible for global warming. Most of these destructive practices persist for economic reasons—to find alternatives is assumed to be too costly.

This presents Christians with a new challenge and a new set of issues. Assuring survival in the biosphere gets added as a social imperative. A growing segment of the public is responding to this challenge—perhaps too slowly. Many Christians are part of that response, but their social concern has not been without its detractors, frequently from the conservative side of the Christian movement.

To blatantly deny the validity of scientific information about global warming may have far more threatening consequences than to repudiate the theory of evolution.

An Alternative Stance

Most forms of social Christianity accept the legitimacy of Christian participation in social and political affairs. They presume that the use of coercive means (whether as legislated mandates, legitimate use of coercive force, or even nonviolent persuasion) to affect social change is necessary. But not all Christians regard such measures as legitimate, and some argue that the use of power and influence to deal with "the world" is a contradiction of the gospel ethic. These Christians are committed to a different way of understanding how Christians should relate to society. This view harks back to the left wing of the Reformation, which understood the relationship between Christian faith and public conduct quite differently than the mainline groups rooted in the Calvinistic and Anglican branches of the Reformation. This approach is now being espoused even by some who do not identify with that left wing tradition. It has been advocated in recent times in *Resident Aliens: A Provocative Christian Assessment of Culture and Ministry for People who Know Something is Wrong*—a small paperback written by Stanley Hauerwas and William Willimon, both connected to Duke University when they wrote the book.

The ideas set forth in this book can be understood as juxtapositions to both the idealism of the Social Gospel and the realism of its Niebuhrian critics. These authors acknowledge the discrepancy between the practices of contemporary society and the moral guidelines of the gospel. But unlike the Social Gospel, they do not suggest that it is feasible to transform society as a whole into a Christian commonwealth. Similarly, they do not adopt the suggestion of Christian realists that we follow the Augustinian scheme for bringing justice to this world through the use of political and social strategies adopted from this world. Rather, Christians are to live as faithfully as they can according to the norms of the gospel as set forth in the Bible—primarily the New Testament—and as exemplified most adequately (though not perfectly) by traditions such as the Mennonites. Hauerwas was attracted to this point of view by years of association with the Mennonite theologian John Howard Yoder when they were teaching together at Notre Dame University.

To live in this manner it is essential to participate in a church whose life is guided by the Sermon on the Mount—in which frugality and a commitment to nonviolence replace the allure of affluence and reliance on violence that are the prominent marks of contemporary society. Doing this becomes a means of serving society by providing it with an example of a better way—a witness that refuses to compromise with society in order to be effective within it. According to Hauerwas making that witness is the only appropriate way of influencing society. This is not a form of withdrawal for the sake of preserving moral innocence but of differentiating behavior so as to demonstrate a patient and loving engagement with the world in order to exemplify a better way.

If this brief set of characterizations is correct, we presently have several rather than merely one kind of Christian concern for society and its well-being. We have an idealistic form that believes society itself can be transformed through religiously motivated goodwill associated with the Enlightenment; we have a realist version that believes justice and well-being must be attained through the use of political and social strategies indigenous to society itself even if they involve compromise with Christian ideals; we have a counter movement that focuses on individual behavior as the best contribution to public life though it may unwittingly embrace a social Darwinism that puts freedom and economic self-interest above concern for justice; and we have the suggestion that by living in a way that is consistent with the gospel ethic of love, self-giving, and nonviolence, Christians can witness to a better way than that of the world. It may be no small wonder that Christian social concern has trouble getting traction in present contemporary American culture.

Dealing with this situation will be a challenge for Christianity well into the foreseeable future. The prospect that these different ways of thinking about the Christian's moral role in society will come to some common stand in the foreseeable future is minimal at best. Perhaps that cancels out the significance of Christianity as a source of social well-being, or maybe it suggests the need for further reflection on the possibility that each may have something to contribute and more than one stance is needed to make a Christian presence in society as meaningful as it is meant to be.

FIVE

Rethinking Ecclesiastical Patterns

Many people are beginning to doubt whether the patterns of church life that have been typical of most Christianity since about the fourth century can or ought to be sustained. Some believe that many Christian practices as now carried on are inconsistent with the way Christianity was first embraced—that special buildings, a designated clerical class, and establishment status (such as participation in public ceremonies, tax exemption, and endorsement of society's use of power) no longer make sense, if indeed they ever were justified. They regard these as the remnants of an outmoded and dysfunctional Christendom. Others, finding it hard to maintain large edifices and paid staff with dwindling memberships are thinking about the need for new patterns of Christian fidelity—patterns that are less costly, more flexible, and oriented to service and witness rather than institutional maintenance. Whether the reason for thinking about new ways of being Christian stems from theological considerations or from a more pragmatic realization that traditional ways of doing things are no longer sustainable, the results can be quite similar: new suggestions for being the church.

The approaches that stem out of these concerns differ from the individualism that merely declares itself to be spiritual but not religious. They are oriented around the idea of deliberately formed communities. They acknowledge that faith must be expressed in some kind of recognizable practice, even though that practice may change from time to time and that we are living in a time when such changes are inescapable. Three versions of this approach are sufficiently identifiable to deserve to be mentioned—though the extent to which they have acquired distinctive features varies. Interestingly, each of these ways uses the term "church" to describe itself—though with a modifier that makes it clear that something new and different is being advocated as a pattern for Christian identity.

House Churches

The first of these patterns is the house church movement. A house church is a group of Christians—of necessity small in size—who meet regularly in the home of one of its members for fellowship and prayer. According to the House Church Resource website there are over 112 million Christians worldwide who are practicing Christianity in this way. That figure may not have the reliability of statistics kept by connectional denominations, but there is no question this movement is significant in size, growing, and attractive to many adherents.

House church Christians believe their practice is consistent with the way Christians gathered for the first three centuries, before the development of the hierarchically structured church. In some countries this movement has taken root because institutional forms of religious activity are frowned upon or banned, but in other countries this movement grows because people are disillusioned with, or unmoved by, traditional institutional practices.

These small groups may or may not have a designated leader, but even if they do the leader derives standing from the group itself and not necessarily from having had special training or having been given special authority by ordination. This tends to minimize, if not eliminate, the significance of ordination as a mark of leadership. There is no doubt some leaders of this sort may possess competence in understanding and interpreting the faith, but they need not pass tests of certification or conform to some measure of right belief in order to exercise a leadership role. This can open Christian practice up to individuals exhibiting self-styled charisma on a small scale, even as mega-churches make a place for doing so on a massive scale.

Undoubtedly the supportive interaction between individuals afforded by the house church model can be both appealing and valuable. The atmosphere in many large congregations can be distant and off-putting—adding to rather than overcoming the sense of isolation and estrangement often characteristic of much contemporary society. Who does not cherish and appreciate supportive intimacy, especially if it is absent from the work-a-day world? Moreover, to maintain this kind of Christian practice is far less expensive than to maintain special buildings, a paid leadership, and connective denominational structures.

To be sure, their use of the Bible provides some assurance that these groups have some substantive Christian orientation. But the use of the Bible alone does not always result in a most profound grasp of theological perspectives, nor does it always guarantee responsible behavior. If the house church movement is to become the future of Christianity mechanisms will need to be created to interrelate house church groups to one another so as to offset the tendency to become an isolated enclave in which the understanding and practice of the gospel takes a merely local configuration. Despite all the misuses and shortcomings that have resulted from the institutionalization of Christianity over the years, it is an important feature of Christian history with beneficial as well as problematic results.

The Emergent Church Movement

A second way of rethinking the church and its role is driven by a conviction that a massive reconceptualizing of Christianity is taking place in the present time out of which there will emerge a new set of revitalized patterns for Christian belief and action. This often amounts to a set of observations about conditions that seem to point toward the need for change rather than a clear vision of what

The Nature and Future of Christianity

is likely to be the shape of the future. But that does not diminish its importance for thinking about the nature and future of Christianity.

The term "the emerging church" can be viewed as an umbrella designation for a variety of efforts to address the need for, and probability of, new ways of thinking and acting. Most of these efforts stem from a realization that there is a deep and growing disenchantment with traditional ways of being church, yet there exists a continuing and even growing hunger for what religious faith can offer those who are destined to live in a modern, technological, commercial, and global culture—many aspects of which fail to support a humane and morally positive way of living. This movement is not aligned directly with any specific group or defined by any presently formulated theological position, but it highlights the importance of an expectant openness to ways in which Christianity can take on new forms and practices.

Perhaps the most erudite, descriptive advocacy of this way of thinking about the emergent church is the book by Phyllis Tickle *The Great Emergence: How Christianity is Changing and Why*. According to Tickle Christianity has undergone crucial reformulations ("attic cleanings") approximately every five hundred years. Her list of these events starts with the work of Gregory the Great as the stabilizing figure in the sixth century; the Great Schism between Eastern and Western forms of Catholicism in the eleventh century; and the Protestant ("Great") Reformation of the sixteenth century. Since it has been about another five hundred years since the Reformation of the sixteenth century there is good reason to assume a major change is now due to occur again. In her discussion of these events Tickle highlights the interplay between religious beliefs and the cultural dynamics of the time and how that interplay has consequences for religious life.

In calling attention to the pressures that are now causing a major reconfiguration of Christian belief and practice Tickle considers the development of so-called modernity—highlighting the challenges to theology posed by Darwin, Freud, and similar figures. She then suggests that the rise of radio and television brought many new ideas to the public consciousness and undercut the plausibility of Christian claims to have an exclusive grasp of truth by enlarging

Rethinking Ecclesiastical Patterns

people's awareness of other places and cultures. Tickle continues her treatment of the factors prompting a new reformulation of Christianity by citing the effect of Einstein's thinking (along with that of Heisenberg) on our understanding of the physical world.

> Out of the mathematics of general relativity would come ideas and postulates that are matters now of household conversations: time as another and fourth dimension; time as capable of being slowed; the ongoing expansion of the universe; the Big Bang. And in conjunction with the work of other brilliant, popularly known physicists, like Edwin Hubble, general relativity would eventually make it possible on July 20, 1969, for Neil Armstrong and Buzz Aldrin to walk on the surface of the Earth's moon. In doing so, they walked on what had always been the footstool of God, and that made all the difference. Literalism, based on inerrancy could not survive the blow (though it would die a slow and painful death); and without inerrancy-based literalism, the divine authority of Scripture was decentralized, subject to the caprices of human interpretation, turned into some kind of pick and choose bazaar for skilled hagglers. Where now is our authority?[1]

The intellectual developments posed by those momentous consequences were not the only pressures on traditional views of religious authority. The twentieth century also saw the rise of Pentecostalism, with its reliance upon the immediacy of the Spirit, together with a revival of speaking in tongues. In the wider culture the development of the automobile—especially in America—as a possession of all but a few individuals undermined the geographically defined parish as the locus of religious activity; religions other than Christianity came to be practiced by friends and neighbors. Drug culture gained a footing. Women's roles in both society and the sanctuary grew. The public's knowledge of the Bible severely diminished despite the learned contributions provided by higher criticism of the Bible. The assault of these and many other pressures of modernity are working together to require the reconfiguration of Christian belief and practice.

---

1. Tickle, *The Great Emergence*, 82.

The Nature and Future of Christianity

In discussing the ecclesiastical patterns that have resulted, Tickle provides four categories by which to characterize the different patterns that are typical of much twentieth century Christianity: the liturgical type (represented for the most part by Roman Catholics and Anglicans); the social justice type (her rubric for most mainline denominations); the revivalist types (charismatics and Pentecostals); and a conservative type (represented by fundamentalists). According to Tickle the lines between these groups are shifting, as are denominational identities. Many Christians belong to groups that espouse two or more of these features. This tends to blur the distinctions between groups that identify themselves doctrinally and those that define themselves behaviorally—producing a new center in which many strands of Christian belief and practice are amalgamated into quite unprecedented approaches, rendering older distinctions unimportant, if not indeed invisible. Thus, in her view,

> American religion had never had a center before, primarily because it was basically Protestant in its Christianity; and Protestantism with its hallmark characteristic of divisiveness, has never had a center. Now one was emerging, but what was emerging was no longer Protestant. It was no longer any "thing" actually. It was simply itself, a mélange of "things" cherry picked from each quadrant [the four groups described above] and put together—some would say cobbled together—without any original intention and certainly with no design beyond that of conversation.[2]

This development has not happened without protest and backlash—backlash that affects the practices of each of the four groups. New forms are emerging—house churches for example, and groups that are "post-modern, post-denominational, post-rational, post-Enlightenment, post-literate, post-almost everything else that only a century before we had been, including post Christendom."[3] Persons attracted to these new forms gladly abandon the old forms, to which they have neither the means nor the desire to return.

2. Ibid., 134.
3. Ibid., 136.

Tickle believes we can identify certain characteristics as the result of this process. In it orthodoxy (right belief) and orthopraxis (right practice) is more fluid though not entirely absent. But their significance will be overshadowed by "Orthonomy, which may be defined then as a kind of 'correct harmoniousness' or beauty."[4] This makes a place for the aesthetic as a means of discerning the truth. Many emergents, she suggests, are impatient with modernist wrestling with questions of historicity—for example, preoccupation with whether or not the virgin birth as a biological event ever took place.

The emergent church movement comes in some less informed and less erudite versions. But all of them would concur with Brian McLaren that modern society is in a state of disarray that fails to support or even harms human life and that "if there is a force in the world powerful enough and good enough to overcome the grinding, destructive momentum of the suicide machine, it is to be found, not in organized religion seeking institutional self-preservation, but in religion organizing for the common good."[5] Overall, emphasis on the emergent church as a means of making human life better suggests that the way in which the emergent church is generally envisioned may still be closer to the social justice type identified by Tickle than to any of the other three patterns.

The Missional Church

The third version of rethinking the nature and function of Christian practice goes by the name "missional church," though one can also hear phases like "missional approach" and "missional living." Although the term "missional" refers to several ways of rethinking the role and function of the community of Christian believers, all of these ways reflect a conviction that the church is called to be a missionary to the culture in which it is located. This conviction differs from the popular idea that missionary work means carrying

---

4. Ibid., 149.
5. McLaren, *Everything Must Change*, 265.

the message of the gospel to cultures that have not heard it or are without Christian institutions.

Missional thinking directs attention toward getting the cultures where Christianity already has a following to take an entirely new look at what it means to profess and practice Christianity. Its advocates perceive that the essence of Christianity has either been forgotten or repudiated in many of the places that consider themselves Christian. The secularism that surrounds most people in the so-called modern world is as much in need of hearing the gospel as are any groups that have supposedly never heard the gospel. Moreover, even those who have tacit and conventional allegiance to Christianity stand in the same need of hearing the gospel as those who have never heard it. This calls for something like evangelism's emphasis on conversion, but involves a great deal more than asking people to accept Jesus Christ as their personal savior.

This means that the church must confront modern culture as a whole, pointing out its pride, fear, greed, and systemic injustices and well as its failure to nurture personal and group well-being. It means confronting the sham and the shame of modern society—even of free societies allegedly governed democratically on Christian principles. Thinking about the role of the church in this way involves a double thrust. While it acknowledges the need for the church to change—to overcome its lethargic bondage to a culture in which Christian values, sensitivities, and practices are either shunned by default or repudiated by choice—it nevertheless believes that the church can proclaim a message of promise to that same society. Missional thinking, therefore, starts with the prophetic task of criticizing the present state of society—particularly of its North American versions that think of themselves as Christian—and shows how much their behavior differs from a Christian vision of communal well-being. But after doing that it goes on to articulate an alternative.

The urgency and complexity of this task is described thoroughly in a book written jointly by a small group of theologians who met to reflect on the claim of this agenda. This book, *Missional Church: A Vision for the Sending of the Church in North America*, combines chapters that diagnose the predicament of modern

Rethinking Ecclesiastical Patterns

societies with affirmations of a Christian alternative. The authors understand this to be a group vocation rather than an individual calling. As they put it,

> A missional ecclesiology must clearly identify and resist all attempts to equip the church merely for its maintenance and security. It must reject every proposal to restore the trappings and privileges of Christendom. It must boldly question every temptation to indulge in compromises with worldly power and jeopardize the institutional practices of servanthood after the model of Jesus. Whenever we see that we are structuring ourselves to serve national, ethnic, or cultural interests, we need to turn to Scripture and to the global church for guidance and correction. Wherever we or our sister communions see the resurgence of our old addictions to control, to management and planning God's future, to strategies to bring in the kingdom, we need humbly to seek God's strength to liberate us. The gospel of the inbreaking reign of God must be upheld as the sole criterion of the particular and connecting structures of the church. That Gospel requires of the church that it be open to surprise, to testing, to suffering, as well as to the blessing of joy and peace.[6]

Needless to say, this is a momentous challenge to achieve a form of Christian fidelity that has few if any historical precedents and few if any outstanding contemporary expressions.

Many of the suggestions raised by the movements described in this chapter raise vexing issues for establishment Christianity. Western Christianity has built both edifices that have played and still play symbolic roles and organizations that carry on programmatic functions—both of which serve cultural needs and require financial resources to continue. Are the functions played by such manifestations of faith without significance and can they be allowed to deteriorate or dissolve without momentous consequences for the relationship between faith and culture? To be sure, when from disuse or malfunction the traditional patterns fail as instruments that

---

6. Guder, *Missional Church*, 268.

advance Christian values, something needs to be done to rectify that condition. In rethinking the role and function of ecclesiastical institutions and practices it is impossible to avoid considering what is gained and what is lost by letting cathedrals turn into mere tourist attractions and doing away with organized structures that relate individual Christians and individual congregations to one another in organized ways.

SIX

Interrelating Traditions

Many years ago, H. Richard Niebuhr, who was then teaching at Elmhurst College, wrote an influential book *The Social Sources of Denominationalism*. The thesis of the book was that the splintering of Christianity—especially of its so-called Protestant side—had come about more for social and political reasons than because of theological disagreements. That contention flew in the face of the common assumption that the divisions within Christianity reflected contrasting doctrinal positions, which people had dug their heals in to defend because religious convictions make people intolerant.

Niebuhr highlighted the fact that Christianity is a deeply divided religion—often for reasons having little to do with deep faith understandings. Most of the approaches that we have been looking at in the previous chapters have done very little to alleviate this condition of divisiveness, and they have possibly added to it. To be sure, Taizé and Iona have sought to bridge the divides between various church traditions and the Social Gospel sought unity on moral rather than doctrinal or institutional grounds. But the fact that Christians are divided remains true, and it is a stumbling block to the church's effectiveness and a target of ridicule from its detractors.

In this chapter we will look at various approaches that focus on relating traditions to one another. Like much else in religious life these approaches have been undergoing changes. Both social

The Nature and Future of Christianity

and doctrinal differences have worked to create divisions; they have also, at times, prompted efforts to overcome them. Clearly there are strong reasons for seeking to relate traditions to one another and, if possible, to bring them into a harmonious and creative relationship. Critics of Christianity are often quick to point out that its divisions, rather than as evidence that religion has the capacity to bring people together, are evidence that religion is a source of antagonism and even of hostility—a fact that we as Christians deny at the price of lost credibility.

Christianity Divided

Christianity has experienced two massive divisions in the course of its history. The first of these was formally declared in 1054 when it divided into Eastern Orthodoxy and Western Orthodoxy (later designated Roman Catholicism). This split was the outcome of centuries of both theological disagreements and cultural differences between the churches in the western part of Europe and the churches in the eastern regions. These differences included alternative views about Christ's nature, disagreements concerning the requirement for clerical celibacy, and perhaps even more importantly, how religious and civil authorities should relate to each other. In the early years of our country, and even perhaps well into more modern times, this division was probably not on the radar of the average American because Eastern Christianity in any of its several subsequent forms had only a small presence in the American religious scene compared to Roman Catholicism. But that is no longer quite as true, and a drive through any large city is likely to go by one or more churches connected to Eastern forms of orthodoxy (usually identifiable by "onion" type roofs). There were no Orthodox students in my seminary class in the forties, but my very first doctoral student at Drew came from this tradition and has subsequently made significant contributions to contemporary theological reflection having value for all believers.

The other major division within Christianity took place in Europe in the sixteenth century. Theological differences were very

Interrelating Traditions

much involved in creating the breach with the Roman Church known as the Protestant Reformation, though they may not explain all the particular reasons for the rupture that took place. The Reformation on the continent was itself complex. It had a left wing component that was as much at odds with figures such as Luther and Calvin as it was with the Roman Church. Fewer theological differences were operative in the case of the English Reformation, which cynics like to point out occurred mainly because a king was unhappy with the Church's treatment of his marital inclinations. Most American denominations trace themselves back to one of the conflicting parties in the events of the past—often adopting outlooks that characterize one of the two orthodoxies of the eleventh century or one of the branches of the Reformation of the sixteenth century.

All of this may seem like ancient and now irrelevant history but it does affect contemporary church life in curious ways. Those ways are not necessarily reflective of the dynamics that created the denominations in the first place but that does not mean they have no contemporary impact on religious loyalties and identities. On the local level denominational differences are now only occasionally understood in terms of their heritage or characterized by differences in doctrine. For instance, years ago, when I was serving as the minister to students at the Presbyterian Church in Blacksburg, Virginia, a couple came to me for advice as to whether or not to join the Episcopal or the Presbyterian Church. One of them belonged to one denomination, the other to the other. Quite rightly, they wanted to experience church membership together. I think they hoped I would give them a long set of profound theological reasons for deciding which denomination was most appropriate—after all, I was teaching religion at the university. Instead, I observed that they were well educated, financially affluent enough, and sufficiently high brow (I think I said "snotty") to feel at home in either congregation. What they needed to decide was whether or not they wished to associate with the cocktail crowd or the tea drinkers. (That difference would be far less applicable today.) My reply—it may have been a Richard Niebuhr type answer—shocked them a bit and they went to the Episcopal church.

The Nature and Future of Christianity

What might I have said to give this couple a theologically informed comparison of these two denominations? The most obvious answer is probably the common assumption that the doctrine of predestination is the main defining mark of Presbyterians. But article seventeen in the Episcopal Book of Common Prayer is a bold a statement of this very same doctrine. Of course, most Episcopalians will assure you they no longer hold to that seemingly harsh belief. And if you know your history of Presbyterianism you will realize that one of its General Assemblies once made a declaration that the doctrine of predestination is not to be understood as contradicting the idea of God's love for all his children. Does this mean the couple had a choice between a denomination that no longer believes what its prayer book says, or a denomination that admits what it believes doesn't mean what it says? That might have thrown them for an even greater loop. So much then for historical background and for mischievous debunking, and for showing how difficult it is to give the current divisions within Christianity neat explanations that carry decisive significance.

Movements for Christian Unity

The efforts to reduce or to overcome divisions within the Christian household were prominent features of twentieth century Christianity. They constitute what is called the ecumenical impulse. This impulse once played a larger role in the religious scene than it may be doing currently. One form it took consisted of efforts to nurture greater cooperation among different Christian bodies while another form sought to do away with denominational divisions—efforts that sometimes only resulted in the creation of new denominations.

At a conference in Edinburgh, Scotland in 1910 many denominations convened to give attention to three matters: The first was the need to avoid duplication and competition between the denominations on the mission field; the second, how to deal with the difference in beliefs and governance that had developed between the different denominations; and the third, how the witness of Christianity to the world could be rendered more consistent and effective.

Interrelating Traditions

Just two years before the Edinburgh Conference, the Federal Council of Churches of Christ had been formed in the United States. The main focus of concern for this organization was on life and work (that is, on Christian practice), and it was influential in the support and advocacy of so-called Social Gospel as described in chapter 4. In a 1950 meeting in Cleveland, Ohio, the Federal Council of Churches merged with seven other program-oriented interdenominational agencies to form the National Council of Churches. This new group had twenty-five Protestant denominations and four Eastern Orthodox communions as members, but it was boycotted by both the fundamentalists (especially the Southern Baptist Convention) and the Roman Catholic Church. The activities of this group expanded, and Rockefeller money enabled it to build new headquarters at 475 Riverside Drive in New York, depriving Barnard College of its outdoor tennis courts and Union Seminary of its view of the Hudson River. The building is hardly an architectural gem and is teasingly referred to those who live and work in the vicinity as "The God Box."

While these developments were taking place in the United States similar efforts to devise ecumenical cooperation were being made in the rest of the world, though primarily in Europe. Many meetings were held, starting in earnest in the 1920s, all seeking to advance the idea of ecumenical unity. The proposal to form a World Council of Churches was agreed to in 1937, but the outbreak of the Second World War delayed the actual implementation of the idea for eleven years. Finally, delegates from 137 church bodies assembled in Amsterdam in 1948 to formally implement the creation of this body. This organization includes almost all Eastern Orthodox groups and most Protestant denominations. From the very beginning student groups had an important role to play in furthering this process. They had held a meeting in Amsterdam in 1939, under the clouds of war, to advance the idea. Although the Roman Catholic Church has not been an official member it does maintain a Pontifical Commission on Christian Unity, which sends observers to the meetings. The headquarters of the World Council of Churches was established in Geneva, Switzerland, and its work since has played a pivotal role in the Christian movement for several decades.

The Nature and Future of Christianity

Needless to say the immense time and effort given to these movements for Christian cooperation stemmed from a belief that such unity is important for the future of Christianity.

There are those who contend that these efforts at cooperation between autonomous denominations did not go far enough—that the principle of federation that is involved is only a partial expression of unity. These persons have pushed for more structural forms of unity—forms that will actually unite churches in functional cohesion rather than settle for merely cooperative activities between otherwise autonomous and separate entities. The effort to achieve more organic unity has taken different paths. One of these has been to unite two or more denominations into a new unity. The clearest example of this is the formation of the United Church of Christ in 1957, which brought together the evangelical reformed and congregational denominations. The title of the new entity may seem to suggest this has accomplished more than actually happened; the resulting union has created a new denomination among other denominations rather than creating any overall healing of the divisions in the Christian movement as a whole. There have also been reunions of northern and southern divisions of denominations spilt apart by the war between the states, the most sizable of these have been the reuniting of the Methodist and the Presbyterian groups.

In 1960 a proposal was initiated to work toward a more organic form of unity. The result was the formation in 1962 of the Consultation on Church Union (COCU), which for years explored ways to bring about greater unity between the members—which were chiefly mainline Protestant denominations. While the work of this group did much to raise the consciousness of people about the burden of their divisions and the possible value of achieving greater unity, the plan of Union it proposed in 1970 failed to gain approval. The sticking point was the matter of church governance and more particularly the basis on which to legitimize the ordaining of ministers across denominational lines so they could validly celebrate at the Eucharist, or Lord's Supper.

Interrelating Traditions

In 2002 this agenda was turned over to a new group, called Churches Uniting in Christ (CUIC). This organization has continued to struggle with the challenge of bringing different denominations to the point where they recognize the legitimacy of each other's ministries, so that the Eucharist might be celebrated in any church by any minister with good standing in his or her denomination. This ideal has not been achieved. However, members of CUIC have taken some steps to facilitate more effective interaction between the various denominations: These include an explicit acknowledgment that all churches are authentic expressions of fidelity to Jesus Christ; recognition that the ministries in the various groups have valid sacramental powers and adhere to Scripture; and agreement as to mission (with special emphasis on overcoming racism). The practical effect of this effort would be to enable ministers to move rather freely from denomination to denomination just as lay members can (with few exceptions). Presently, there are at present a lot of technical and sometimes seemingly arbitrary barriers to doing that. CUIC hoped those barriers would be overcome by 2007, but many are still there—sometimes honored in the breach as well as in the observance. Individual officials of various denominations sometimes permit clergy of other groups to participate in the sacramental life of their own communion by winking at the technicalities that still prove barriers to full intercommunion.

Interest in the ecumenical endeavors of the last century is waning, not only among those who do not think they went far enough, but also among those who do not feel all this effort is sufficiently important to occupy much time and effort. But there are more significant and sobering indicators of the decline. The staff of the National Council of Churches once stood at four hundred members. By 2012 it had less than twenty and was still shrinking. Churches Uniting in Christ has closed its office. The existence and work of the World Council of Churches seems to enjoy much less attention and support among American Christians than it did some years ago.

This does not mean nothing is happening. Many communities have ministerial associations or councils of churches that do things together. Both clergy and laity often work together to meet human need or to devise services for special occasions rather than develop a common understanding of the faith. The liturgical forms from Taizé are prominently used by such groups. Most joint services are likely to celebrate civic events, such as Thanksgiving, and can therefore take place without posing the sticky issue of joint communion. Ecumenical cooperation has still not been very successful in resolving the question as to who is legitimately qualified to authorize or to celebrate that sacrament. For some denominations, such as the United Church of Christ, the validity of ordination and the reservation of the Eucharist to its own members isn't an issue—but for others, such as the Missouri Synod Lutherans and the Roman Catholics, these matters are a major source of concern. Some agreements have been reached between individual denominations moving toward the mutual recognition of ministries. Illustrative of these agreements is an agreement between the Episcopalians and the ELCA (Evangelical Lutheran Church of America) to recognize each other's ministries and another between the Lutherans and the Presbyterians to do the same. This has had some ironic consequences, namely that the Lutherans can serve as ministers in any of the three churches, but Episcopalians and Presbyterians can't. Some recent efforts to overcome that strange situation have come up with a mutual recognition between Presbyterians and Episcopalians, but with the limitation that Presbyterians can now celebrate the Eucharist in an Episcopal church but cannot use the form in the Book of Common Prayer to do so.

The Shift Toward an Interfaith Perspective

With the development of globalization it has become increasingly clear that Christianity is only one religion among many others. This raises problems for the view that Christianity is the only true and proper response to God. Many Christians are finding ways to incorporate aspects of other religious traditions into their practice of Christianity. In some respects this concern has much greater significance in a world dominated by tensions and conflicts between colliding cultures than it does for ecumenical cooperation between

Interrelating Traditions

groups within one faith tradition. What might come as a bit of surprise is that the interfaith idea has an even earlier start than the ecumenical agenda.

In Chicago in 1893, in conjunction with the World Columbian Exposition (a precursor to World Fairs) a group of religious leaders from around the world met as the first World's Parliament of Religions. This is frequently cited as the first instance of interfaith dialogue. It was organized under the leadership of an American clergyman, John Henry Barrows, and it met for sixteen days. Some religious groups were absent, among them Native Americans and Sikhs, but some new religious movements such as Christian Science were included. The gathering was addressed by Swami Vivekananda, who represented Hinduism and based his appeal for interfaith understanding on passages from the Bhagavad Gita. Vivekananda was a student of the great Hindu religious pluralist Ramakrishna who contended that all religions lead to God, though the exact form of God cannot be specified. Vivekananda appeared in an orange robe and a saffron turban. One of the central themes of his short speech was a call for the renunciation of religious intolerance and sectarian violence—a stance that set him clearly at odds with the thinking of militant Muslims, such as Sayyid Quitb (KOOTub) in Egypt, and many representatives of just becoming American fundamentalism. This meeting was prompted in large measure by what was then just becoming an awareness of the global nature of the human enterprise.

Although the interfaith movement started back then it did not get much traction for quite some time. Then, a century later, eight thousand people met again at the Palmer House in Chicago using the same title for their meeting. This time the opening keynote address was given by Dr. Gerald Barney of the Millennium Institute using a document inspired by the Roman Catholic theologian Hans Kung that argued the case for a global ethic. The closing keynote was delivered by the Dalai Lama, and Cardinal Joseph Bernardin was a participant. The World's Parliament of Religion met again in 1999 in Cape Town, South Africa, and in 2004 in Barcelona, Spain. The 2004 meeting highlighted four themes: mitigating religiously motivated violence, ensuring access to safe water, dealing with

The Nature and Future of Christianity

the fate of refugees worldwide, and eliminating the external debt of developing countries. The agenda of this movement included considerable attention to ethical considerations and social justice. This seemed a plausible foundation for cooperation at the time. Still another meeting of the World's Parliament of Religion took place in Melbourne, Australia in 2009. That meeting lasted six days and addressed issues of global climate change and environmental sustainability. The meeting was a sign that despite continuing religious differences the global nature of the human enterprise was starting to be acknowledged and that religion needed to recognize that change in outlook.

The task of achieving interfaith cooperation may be far more complex and difficult than is sometimes recognized. It is not enough to simply decide to be friends. Perhaps the deepest problem is that every major religious tradition is itself divided between those with moderate outlooks favorable to cooperation and those insisting on making exclusive claims for their own tradition that may even entail holding all others in contempt. Intransigence is found in part of every major faith community and produces division even within those separate households. And if it is not easy to overcome such stances even within a group of supposedly shared beliefs, what are the prospects for dealing with divisions between religious communities with widely differing histories, priorities, and beliefs?

In his book, *Beyond Tolerance*, Professor Gustav Niebuhr, who teaches religion at Syracuse University, makes two points: 1) many efforts to achieve interfaith understanding are local in nature (where face-to-face encounter is possible), and 2) the academic teaching of religion has made significant contributions to interfaith understanding—especially when it involves field trips to sacred places of different traditions. Those trips must be prepared with skill and conducted by knowledgeable leaders. Otherwise, interfaith cooperation will be little more than a quasi-baptized version of mere curiosity.

The quest for understanding needs to pay attention to deep, crucial, and inescapable differences that are the defining features

Interrelating Traditions

of individual traditions. Alternative ideas concerning the nature of God, the enigma of the human condition, and the content of morality and spirituality have to be understood and acknowledged. Conceptual differences do matter and cannot be superficially overlooked in order to achieve congeniality. When large majorities of persons in any of the major faith traditions don't even understand their own heritage in depth, the problem of bringing responsible understanding of how faith traditions can cooperate is rather daunting. Experiences associated with belonging to just one faith tradition are too easily deemed normal and universal. To be sure, enormous strides have been made in understanding religion as an academic field. A considerable part of this enlarged understanding involves learning about the beliefs and practices of other cultures and traditions, thus seeming to facilitate interfaith understanding. But those strides are often overlooked by people in their local and parochial institutions. Hopefully that condition will be remedied in time.

Two other examples of interfaith efforts deserve mention. One is a growing number of arrangements for dialogue between the three Abrahamic faiths—Judaism, Christianity, and Islam. While this may be a somewhat narrower focus than the agenda of the meetings of the World's Parliament of Religion, it still is worth pursuing. The Claremont School of Theology in California—a Methodist Seminary—has joined with the Academy of Jewish Religion of California and the Islamic Center of Southern California to create new Claremont Lincoln University where equal numbers of Jews studying to be Rabbis, Christians studying to be ministers, and Muslims studying to be Imams are preparing in the same institution for leadership in their respective traditions. The Presbyterian Conference ground at Stony Point, New York is trying to create and sustain that same kind of dialogue on a much less ambitious scale.

The other example of interfaith interest is the effort on the part of a few seminary professors to become fully conversant with at least one other religious tradition and in some cases to actually live as practicing believers in two communities. Such persons are relatively few in number and they often are subject to not inconsiderable suspicion as to their suitability as faculty members in denominationally related seminaries. In one instance, a seminary had a faculty member who had become a Voodoo priestess following her initial appointment. Some, like the dean who came after her initial appointment, contended this disqualified her to be a member of a Christian seminary faculty; others contended that this meant she could be especially effective in making future clergypersons face up to the realities of religious pluralism.

The interfaith movement has made considerable use of the document *A Global Ethic: The Declaration of the Parliament of the World's Religion.* It did seem for many during the rise of both the ecumenical movement and interfaith initiatives that agreement about moral matters was easier to achieve than agreement about doctrinal formulations. This was a time when the Ethical Culture Society was flourishing in places like New York City on the premise that people could be brought together around ethical ideals if they bracketed out so-called "overbeliefs." That assumption no longer has obvious plausibility. In his autobiography, Wesley Granberg-Michaelson reflects on the impact of moral disagreements regarding homosexuality between first and third world participants in the World Council of Churches and how that difference has made cooperative work difficult and sometimes impossible. In contemporary America the sharp disagreements and antagonisms that we are now experiencing—frequently denoted as cultural warfare—reflect that same change in the religious situation. Common agreement about morality no longer serves to overcome differences.

The future of interfaith movements is difficult to predict. Can such groups furnish the same support and satisfaction as particular traditions? How will they be financed and governed? Who will make judgments as to when interfaith activity is substantive and meaningful and when it is merely ephemeral? That does not preclude approaches that are focused on the transformation of society, but it does make those approaches far less promising as the basis for common agreement than might have been true several years ago.

A comparison between the ecumenical impulse and the interfaith impulse highlights what may be the most interesting question of all. In one the effort tends to be on achieving some commonly accepted practices and beliefs as the basis for unity; in the other the trend is to accept differences and make the acceptance of diversity the goal. Dealing with this contrast as to how religious people can live together and contribute to human well-being may be the challenge that dominates the future.

Concluding Reflections

Embracing Diversity: Being Faithful Modestly

What are we to think of this plethora of alternatives? Do these differences about doctrine, morality, and the nature of the church suggest Christianity has no defining features—that it is understood and practiced in so many ways that its identity is lost? Is it a collection of contrasts, confusions, and contradictions that render it meaningless, or is it a collage of alternative approaches that involve a variety of meaningful responses, each of which has some value as a witness to a more comprehensive outlook?

The answer given to this question will depend a great deal upon how those who respond understand reality and how they look upon religious faith as a source of insight for dealing with that reality. It is possible, perhaps even normal, to assume that understanding must be uniform to be significant, that truth comes only in a single version, that there can be only one form of righteousness. From that perspective differences are viewed as indications of either inadequacies or faults—that unless a single, agreed upon way of understanding or a uniform set of practices is definitive then something is amiss. That assumption is a prevalent one. This view about proper knowing and proper acting—either stated explicitly or merely assumed—is held by many devotees of religion and also by many so-called secularists. This assumption—that uniformity is both possible and necessary for intellectual legitimacy and social health—has enormous appeal, both to persons of faith and to persons of doubt.

But this assumption about the univocal nature of truth has its dangers. It prompts heresy hunts in religion and it creates intolerance toward outsiders in political and social affairs. It remains a part of many modern secular mindsets despite their lip service to openness and tolerance. For instance, views that regard science as providing a single incontrovertible grasp of reality that excludes the role of faith can exhibit the same rigidity as the intolerant forms of religious belief they decry. The assumption that understanding can have only one form is the parent of dogmatism, whether of a religious or nonreligious type.

This way of thinking is now being reconsidered in face of the evidence that a single understanding of reality and social behavior eludes us, in religion just as much as many other aspects of our lives. All human understandings and achievements are limited and partial—the work of human minds and hands with all the limitations that implies. Even when dealing with ultimate matters our conceptions remain limited and partial. None of our understandings are complete or permanent and none of our behaviors are clearly either so good or so evil that it completely eliminates ambiguity from our lives. It may be unsettling to face this condition but it need not be our undoing. It calls for dealing with life by using a different set of assumptions about how to cope with matters of knowing, belief, and practice—one that acknowledges the inevitability of diversity and proceeds to learn and profit from that diversity by studying its complexity and looking beyond to the Reality each alternative attempts to understand, albeit in a limited and partial way.

It is possible to regard diversity as something to be lived with and even appreciated rather than as something that must be entirely overcome in order to think correctly or to live rightly. To think that any of us possesses the whole truth and nothing but the truth is a form of arrogance, the occasion for both creedal and anti-creedal rigidity. But that does not mean we are totally robbed of a glimpse of truth or prevented from having some sense of what is ultimately worthwhile. A limited understanding is possible as well as adequately constructive behavior, and there are various legitimate

Embracing Diversity: Being Faithful Modestly

ways of thinking and acting short of omniscient correctness, especially when dealing with things of greatest importance. To recognize this is not to embrace relativism in the usual sense, since most relativism holds that each and every position is so conditioned by its circumstances that it has little decisive claim upon our understanding. Ironically, that same relativism is often enunciated as a definitive and final word about how to understand things correctly, thus unwittingly exempting itself from its own charge.

To embrace diversity creatively and soberly is a challenge. It involves respect for the views of others and allows for different groups to have their own perspectives and practices by which they define themselves. To be sure, not all alternatives are of equal legitimacy or helpfulness. Differences are not without significance and no position can presume to be exempt from scrutiny. Although nobody possesses complete intellectual understanding or lives with total behavioral responsibility, that is not a license to do away with trying to do the best we can. There may be some truth in every one of the approaches that have been cited in the foregoing text, but there may also be inadequacy, distortion, and even error. Conversations between these possibilities can yield healthy insights, but only if done candidly and in an effort to appreciate and accept both the validity and limitations of the options. While to insist that just one of them is correct is to be mistaken in one way, to repudiate or disconnect from all of them is to be mistaken in another.

This means that we are dependent on being justified by faith in matters of belief and understanding fully as much as in matters of conduct and behavior. We can live with partial understandings just as we live with incomplete virtue. This does not eliminate the need for thoughtful judgment or careful reflection, but it renders the value of that process dependent on grace rather than on complete and final answers from which deviation is apostasy. It is probably more accurate to suggest that this is a way of being faithful modestly than of sinning bravely, but in either case we are enabled to live by grace rather than by impervious correctness. From this stance we are also enabled to see and acknowledge values in the thoughts and action of others who are likewise willing to draw upon the healing and redeeming power of the gospel, even if they do so in different ways.

The Nature and Future of Christianity

This provides significance to the many approaches to the nature and future of Christianity to which this book seeks to call attention and about which it offers evaluative comments.

When we adopt this premise as the foundation for how we think about the matters we have described we can wrestle freely with the task of understanding the nature and future of Christianity. We do not have to know completely what God is like or commit ourselves to just one single account of how God has acted in history. Trust is possible without presumed omniscience; assurance is legitimate on the basis of hope rather than certainty. We can acknowledge that all ideas about the Ultimate are historically derived, that many ways of framing that knowledge have helpful uses, and that any spiritual commitment that altogether denies the possibility of alternatives borders on idolatry. We can guard our thinking against being fully tied to the ways people in the past have wrestled with these matters, but also against being swept up in the embrace of some contemporary alternative. God has spoken important truths, is still speaking new insights, and will speak in unexpected ways in the future. Religion errs if it focuses entirely on just one of these time frames as the source of its convictions—whether by being entirely subservient to received authority, relying completely on immediate inspiration, or presuming to foresee the future with certainty.

This means that new attempts to formulate religious understandings are likely to be most valuable when they enrich and supplement what has been thought in the past rather than when they completely repudiate and overturn it. Growth depends upon having roots but is destroyed when the plant becomes root-bound. Growth is never entirely self-sustaining as if it could occur without nutrients, or take place without being an integral part of an order of being that gives substance to existence. We can no more say to our Source of Being "we have no need of you" than leaves can say that to a plant. But that does not require every leaf to be like every other leaf or every plant to be like every other plant. Diversity in the sphere of biology does not diminish the quality of nature or take away from its grandeur. Why then do some people think it is a threat to religious integrity?

Embracing Diversity: Being Faithful Modestly

What then are weeds? Are they not species that seek to overrun the garden plot with nothing but their own kind? They are not necessarily poisonous (though they can be); they are not necessary ugly (though they can be); they are simply plants that seem to deny other plants to an equal place in the garden. What, then, would constitute a theological weed?

Much religious zeal goes into insisting that there is only one legitimate moral standard to which everyone must conform. That impulse is the incubator of so-called moral legalism, that is, of the view that the task of religion is to advocate conformity of behavior in order to protect the stability of human life. The cultural wars that so sharply divide us often take place between parties that insist some single moral stance must be imperative. How, if at all, can we avoid that predicament and the stalemates it creates?

Attempts to do so can present enormous challenges. There are plenty of moral "weeds"—forms of behavior that if allowed to swamp out all the alternatives would impose harsh and brittle demands for conformity. Is behavior to be measured by some abstract standard set down on tablets of stone or by the dictates of a religious authority, or is it to be judged by how it enriches humankind? Are persistent efforts to control the behavior of others a greater threat to human well-being than behavioral diversity? To pose these questions is to examine the function of religious morality on its most crucial level. Is being righteous merely a form of outward behavior judged by external standards, or is it the cultivation of compassionate attitudes that may serve the good in more than one valid way?

It is easiest, of course, to deal with externally observable behavior. Courts do that primarily, though they sometimes take motives into account regarding the severity of the offense. However, in the legal system determination of motives is not the factor on which judgments on guilt or innocence depend as much as the factor that determines the seriousness of an offense. Legal systems utilize code morality; legislatures can properly prohibit certain forms of misbehavior, but would be out of place passing an ordinance requiring everybody to be happy. In contrast to legal forms of morality,

The Nature and Future of Christianity

religion cannot ignore the matter of intent and motivation. In many respects dealing with that factor is its unique role.

The problems confronting society have deeper roots than the failure of people to line up in support of just one moral position or single political agenda. This is why, in dealing with the relationship of Christianity to society, we must go beyond the assumption that the main role of religion is to support one policy. We need to understand how the principalities and powers that surround us shape our outlooks and exercise control over our passions, and why this prevents the transformations that are needed to render society more humane and responsible.

Behind both the growing development of economic disparities and the threat to the environment that mark much present economic behavior lays greed. In some cases this takes the form of a blatant grasp for financial return on an inordinate scale, but it is not absent from more modest quests for material well-being pursued without regard for their impact on others or on earth. As long as greed is the major motivating impulse for behavior, whatever can be accomplished by policy regulations to control bad practice will be inadequate, and sometimes the regulations may be twisted to protect the very malfunctions they are intended to curb. However, it is wrong to take that as an argument against the use of such regulations, as libertarians often do, for regulations are generally obeyed by those with hearts of flesh and they may help to keep those with hearts of stone from engaging in exploitative behavior. Even so, human nature being what it is, those whose greed is unchecked by a self-restraint rooted in devotion to a higher good will devise ways to thwart all efforts to implement more responsible policies. That is why basic attitudes must be changed if society is to benefit.

Just as we need to turn around the dominance of greed in our handling of resources we need to overcome fear in our approach to domestic and international relationships. Conflicts, coupled with the impulse to use violence to overcome them, seem to be increasing all around us. The fear of violence often drives people to develop the capacity to use counter-violence for protection. The yearning to possess guns for the purposes of protecting the self or loved ones is prompted by fear. As long as fear dominates our consciousness the see-saw relationship between the threat of violence and the threat of counter-violence will continue to intensify. Who knows where it will end?

It may be the role of religion to help people overcome such fear, or at least keep it sufficiently reduced so as to avoid the cauldron of distrust and violence into which we seem to be falling. The challenge involved in doing this is central to the idea of peacemaking. It calls for seeing the world in an alternative way. Fear is often a product of the inability to accept diversity—of the understandable suspicion of the neighbor who differs and with whom there is no interchange. Moreover, fear tends to blind us to the dangers into which our present ways of thinking can lead us. Those, like neighborhood watchmen, who for understandable reasons feel they have to carry weapons in order to protect themselves or their kin, should soberly consider what it would mean to use them. To carry a weapon is to practically foreordain how one will respond to a crisis, but it offers little in the way of solace for the agony that can follow, having done so with the use of lethal force. Legal acquittal doesn't necessarily offer release from the trauma created by having shot another person, even when an act of defense.

To overcome fear in the larger realm of international relationships is equally important but even more difficult. When nations try to make themselves feel safe by making other nations afraid the result is to rely more and more on instruments of violence that create more fear. To help nations break out of this cycle of distrust may be the most significant contribution that religion can make to the world. To date its effectiveness in doing this is disappointedly meager despite the professed allegiance to the ideal of peace that is part of almost every religious tradition.

Because changing such attitudes is crucial, Christian social responsibility depends upon repentance as well as on well-meaning resolves. The place of repentance in Christian fidelity is probably most clearly enunciated by conservatives and evangelicals. However, they often fail to see how it applies to public behavior as well as to individual wrongdoing and thereby overlook its potential value

The Nature and Future of Christianity

for healing society. Rather than merely criticizing the individualism of evangelicals we should be sensitive to the truth to which they can point us. Repentance is the realization that we simply need to recognize that we are doing some things wrongly and open ourselves to the Power than can replace hearts of stone with hearts of flesh. Only when we do that can we benefit from the transformative power of the gospel.

In *An Ethic for Enemies: Forgiveness in Politics*, Donald Shriver provides a solid theological grounding for regarding repentance as significant for the public as well as the private sphere. This has done much to overcome the assumption of many conservatives that repentance has only private significance and also the assumption of many Christian realists, like Reinhold Niebuhr, that large groups—like nation states—find it impossible to undertake. By examining the social healing possible through the work of Truth and Reconciliation Commissions, such as those which took place in South Africa, Shriver has demonstrated in quite convincing ways that the dichotomy between private and public behavior that once was taken as a given can be transcended.

Throughout this overview of the various approaches we have frequently encountered the fact that many people are suspicious of institutional religion in general, not merely critical of one manifestation of it. They often claim to prefer an individually practiced spirituality to organized religion. Their distrust of institutions is similar to the outlook of the Tea Party in contemporary politics—though, somewhat ironically, it usually comes from the ideological left rather than the right. While this reflects an understandable distrust of institutional efforts to impose uniformity by authoritarian means, it is not the same as the endorsement of diversity. One denies the value of interaction with others; the other celebrates it. *E Pluribus Unum* stands for a nation that honors institutionalized ways of protecting differences and bringing them together for common purposes. It does not commend the disjoining of all parties into entirely separate entities.

Embracing Diversity: Being Faithful Modestly

Although institutions, including churches, grow old and do not fully function as they were originally intended, and even at times becoming oppressive, they cannot be simply dispensed with. Better to have many different institutions working to accomplish many different aims than to have none at all. Honoring diversity is compatible with institutionally structured community. It simply warns against letting just one institution become all-controlling. The penchant for the purely private in religion has not yet run its course to the point where a backlash is likely to occur. It may not ever do that in a society where the practice of religion is entirely free and the dangers of one religion becoming excessively controlling are minimal. While freedom of religion often protects even the foolish and the bizarre, at the same time it prevents the oppressive and the unduly authoritarian from taking over. If a religious practice becomes clearly dangerous to others it tends to be curtailed by general consent even if that involves a breach in the separation of church and state. An allegedly religious good cannot be used as a cloak for any malfeasance or behavior that poses a severe threat to the public good.

Some feel that the future of Christianity is, or ought to be, consignment to oblivion. This hostility has been around in some form for as long as Christianity, which has survived despite opposition from without and shortcomings within. Hostility to Christianity takes both passive and strident forms and is frequently associated with distrust of all religion. The claim that Christianity is something else than a religion and therefore exempt from the vicissitudes and problems that are ascribed to that feature of human behavior seems to carry little weight in allaying this opposition. Someday perhaps the expectation that Christianity, along with religion, will bite the dust may prove correct, but that would not cancel out the experience of accepting grace and forgiveness or the challenge to holy living that have provided comfort and challenge to multitudes and that remain crucial to any constructive and enduring response to the majestic wholeness of Being Itself. The Apostle Paul knew this when he wrote:

The Nature and Future of Christianity

For at present we see puzzling reflections in a mirror, but then face to face. At present I know only partially, but then I shall understand fully, even as I have been fully understood.[1]

---

1. 1 Cor 13:12, translated by John D. Elder.

Bibliography

Cone, James H. *A Black Theology of Liberation*. Philadelphia: Lippincott, 1970.

———, and Gayraud S. Wilmore, editors. *Black Theology: A Documentary History*. Maryknoll, NY: Orbis, 1979.

Cox, Harvey. *The Future of Faith*. New York: HarperCollins, 2009.

———. *The Secular City: Secularization and Urbanization in Theological Perspective*. New York: Macmillan, 1965.

de Botton, Alan. *Religion for Atheists: A Nonbeliever's Guide to the Uses of Religion*. New York: Pantheon, 2012.

Gilkey, Langdon. *Message and Existence: An Introduction to Christian Theology*. New York: Seabury, 1979.

Granberg-Michaelson, Wesley. *Unexpected Destinations: An Evangelical Pilgrimage to World Christianity*. Grand Rapids: Eerdmans, 2011.

Guder, Darrell L., editor. *Missional Church: A Vision for the Sending of the Church in North America*. Grand Rapids: Eerdmans, 1998.

Gutierrez, Gustavo. *A Theology of Liberation: History, Politics, and Salvation*. Maryknoll, NY: Orbis, 1972.

Hauerwas, Stanley, and William H. Willimon. *Resident Aliens: A Provocative Christian Assessment of Culture and Ministry for People Who Know that Something is Wrong*. Nashville: Abingdon, 1989.

Kung, Hans, and Karl Josef Kuschel, editors. *A Global Ethic: The Declaration of the Parliament of the World's Religions*. New York: Continuum, 1993.

Lindbeck, George A. *The Nature of Doctrine: Religion and Theology in a Post-Liberal Age*. Philadelphia: Westminster, 1984.

Bibliography

McLaren, Brian D. *Everything Must Change: Jesus, Global Crisis, and a Revolution of Hope.* Nashville: Thomas Nelson, 2007.

National Council of Churches. *A Social Creed for the 21st Century.* http://www.ncccusa.org/news/ga2007.socialcreed.html.

Niebuhr, Gustav. *Beyond Tolerance: Searching for Interfaith Understanding in America.* New York: Viking, 2008.

Niebuhr, H. Richard. *The Social Sources of Denominationalism.* New York: Henry Holt, 1929.

Oden, Thomas C. *After Modernity—What?: Agenda for Theology.* Grand Rapids: Zondervan, 1990.

———. *Agenda for Theology.* New York: Harper & Row, 1979.

———. *Rebirth of Orthodoxy: Signs of New Life in Christianity.* San Francisco: HarperSanFrancisco, 2002.

Osteen, Joel. *Becoming a Better You: 7 Steps to Improving Your Life Everyday.* New York: Free Press, 2007.

———. *Your Best Life Now: 7 Steps to Living at Your Full Potential.* New York: Warner, 2004.

Peale, Norman Vincent. *The Art of Living: A Guide to Confident Thinking.* New York: Abingdon, 1937.

———. *The Power of Positive Thinking.* New York: Prentice-Hall, 1952.

Rauschenbusch, Walter. *A Theology for the Social Gospel.* Reprint. Introduction by Donald W. Shriver, Jr. Louisville: Westminster John Knox, 1997.

———. *Christianity and the Social Crisis.* Reprint. Introduction by Douglas F. Ottati. Louisville: Westminster John Knox, 1997.

Robinson, John A. T. *Honest to God.* Louisville: Westminster John Knox, 1963.

Shriver, Donald W., Jr. *An Ethic for Enemies: Forgiveness in Politics.* New York: Oxford University Press, 1997.

Spong, John Shelby. *A New Christianity for a New World: Why Traditional Faith is Dying and a New Faith is Being Born.* San Francisco: HarperSanFrancisco, 2001.

———. *Why Christianity Must Change.* San Francisco: HarperSanFrancisco, 1998.

Tickle, Phyllis. *The Great Emergence: How Christianity in Changing and Why.* Grand Rapids: Baker, 2008.

Warren, Rick. *The Purpose Driven Life: What on Earth Am I Here For?* Grand Rapids: Zondervan, 2002.

www.ingramcontent.com/pod-product-compliance
Lightning Source LLC
Chambersburg PA
CBHW070513090426
42735CB00012B/2762